Urban Xcellence

Urban Xcellence

*Unveiling Extraordinary Stories by
Everyday People*

Malcom X. Bowser

MOME
PUBLISHING

Urban Xcellence

MOME Publishing Inc.
P.O. Box 24
Bronx, NY 10471
www.UrbanXBook.com
Email: Malcombowser51@gmail.com

ISBN 978-0-9772357-5-9
Library of Congress Control Number 2019914290

Editor: Jessica LeeAnn
Cover design & layout: Latonia Almeyda
Cover concept: Renee Irby

www.UrbanX.NYC   www.UrbanXBook.com
Twitter: @UrbanX_NYC   Twitter: @Top_Xth
IG: @UrbanX_NYC   IG: @Top_Xth

Dedication

This book is dedicated to the people who embrace their community as a gift rather than a curse. To the people who define success by the lives they impact, and not the number on their banking app. To the people who lose sleep because their goals keep them up at night. This book is dedicated to the past, present, and future YOU. #UrbanXcellence

Table of Contents

Foreword

You only live once, so why not be great? I am an award-winning branding architect, #1 best-selling author, and a global motivational speaker. I also serve as CEO of The Brand Executive. It is a company that works with you to assemble plans, strategies, and tools that are unique to your goals, your business, and your industry. I have developed award-winning marketing and social responsibility campaigns, creatively aligned companies with their target audiences and consulted over 1,500 entrepreneurs in strategic brand expansion. I have led consumer-marketing initiatives for a diverse portfolio of brands such as Allstate Insurance Co., U.S. Army, Jay-Z's Roc Nation, McDonald's, Tommy Hilfiger, and Coors Light.

Now, I don't say all of this to brag. The way society is set up, if you don't layout your receipts on the table, people will tune you out because of the vast amounts of information readily available. Not to mention, if you're not on television or a celebrity to the mainstream, your genius almost doesn't exist to them. What is missed by this mindset is the secret to obtaining the golden nuggets or what I call the magic intel — the unconventional path. We currently live in a world where the fake is winning, and it's unfortunate. A lot of misdirection and opinion shared as facts instead of insights and actual fact-finding research.

Early on in my career, I was fortunate in that I would tune out the majority and align with the rare and misrepresented. In doing so, this led to me meeting an incredible soul by the name of Duane Bowser aka The Black Dot. Self-awareness is defined as conscious knowledge of one's own character, feelings, motives, and desires. To identify your purpose and path in life, it truly starts with being in tune with who you are and acknowledging what is meaningful to you. Dot had and still has the ability to walk you down a guided rabbit hole to help you question what needed to be challenged and appreciate life's offerings.

What came from our friendship of 10+ years is a newly birthed friendship between his son, Malcom and I. A fiery, passionate student of life growing into his own in no time. I am a real fan of those who not only talk a good game, but actually put action behind their words, and Malcom has been a man of action consistently. Through Malcom's journey, he has built a reliable media outlet along with Dot in UrbanX TV, which has led us to today – Urban Xcellence.

Urban Xcellence not only highlights and uplifts amazing stories, but this project also defines what Black Excellence can look like and be. This book, through a remarkable halo effect, levels the playing field for those who aren't celebrities, and not on television or radio. Those featured have their message and unique experiences offered for consumption by the masses and leading you directly to their magical intel providing to be applied. With roses come thorns and part of the equation to growth is through trials and tribulations. The beauty of this particular project is Malcom's ability to capture the ups and downs of each unique story and present it in a digestible manner that can, in turn, be applied from crucial learning's.

Be authentic to who you are and work towards creating change in the world. There aren't enough representation for the real, but Urban Xcellence does a fantastic job in defying the norm. Stop chasing the fake and missing the essential steps. Be true to your path and remember there is no need to compare. Your journey is your journey, and it should be celebrated and highlighted for the world to learn and grow. Unique is and always will be the cool.

- Steve Canal. Award winning branding architect, best-selling author, CEO, husband and father.

Introduction

"We are the sum total of our experiences. Those experiences – be they positive or negative – make us the person we are, at any given point in our lives. And, like a flowing river, those same experiences, and those yet to come, continue to influence and reshape the person we are, and the person we become. None of us are the same as we were yesterday, nor will be tomorrow." – **B.J. Neblett**

That quote by B.J. Neblett is one that perfectly encapsulates what the objective is at Urban X. We do not come into this world as fixed beings; it's impossible. Some people may be more stubborn than others (me included) but when we come on to the planet, we are shaped and molded by our choices — and how we react to what happens around us. Thus, we form our opinions, habits and overall personality, making us who we fundamentally are.

My father often refers to the first line when discussing anything past, present, or future. It has shaped my worldview and has helped me at least try to understand other perspectives even when on the surface it may not make sense.

Urban X began in April of 2017. Just as the quote above states, what you hold in your hands is the result of many great books I've read, amazing people I have come in contact with, and my overall experiences in life.

During the spring semester of my junior year in college, I worked as a women's shoe salesman at Macy's. The job wasn't anything special, but as a broke college student I couldn't complain; I was grateful to even have a job.

One Thursday at work I was rushing to clock out so I could meet up with my friends for the campus "festivities", and I saw one of my old professors shopping for shoes with her daughter. She taught my Intro to Journalism course, and while I didn't need to take the class for my degree requirements, I thought the class would be easy enough to fulfill my optional requirements. Despite my intentions for enrolling, I actually enjoyed her class.

I walked over to help her, and she greeted me very warmly. She told me what she needed and I obliged. During the interaction, she asked me if I had taken any more journalism classes. I told her I didn't because I was just getting into many of my more challenging classes for my major. She looked at me and said, "I still stand by what I told you before, you'd make a great journalist." I laughed, rang up her purchase then looked up and saw she was serious. She asked me for a pen, took a piece of receipt paper and wrote down the email address to the head of the Media and Communications department at my school. She said I should reach out to him for internship opportunities. My professor felt that if I got some experience that I would maybe change my mind in the future, plus I would be able to use the credits. That didn't sound like a bad idea to me.

So later that weekend, I emailed the head of the department. He immediately put me in contact with a local newspaper publication that he thought I fit in well with based on the recommendation from my professor. That summer going into my senior year in college, I completed the internship. My duties required me to attend local events, interview people, and write opinion pieces for the newspaper. It was a great experience, and one that taught me a lot about the field. For my final assignment, the head of the publication gave me an opportunity to be the guest editor for the entire paper and online website. She told me I would have control over everything, who writes what, what pictures go where; I was in charge.

That week it felt like I was permanently attached to my seat in front of my laptop with the phone to my ear. I had to search for news, confirm sources, write my own stories, and make sure the rest of the staff had the support they needed. I was stressed out my mind, but I was enjoying myself.

When the paper finally came out, it was a success. All of the hard work I put in paid off.

My friends were slightly taken aback by what I was doing at the internship because it really had nothing to do with my major, which was history. I once had aspirations of working in the museum field as a curator, but after my short stint as the guest editor for the newspaper, I got the bug. I began seeing myself write what I wanted and be able to control the narrative, maybe even start my own publication.

Around the same time that I began to brainstorm ideas, I had just finished reading Hill Harper's book *Letters to a Young Brother* for the third time. My mother gifted it to me and when I finally picked it up, I found so much value in it.

One thing I did notice is that every time I read the book, I was somewhere different in my life — a little older, a little wiser. My overall perspective changed on some of the topics he wrote about. Maybe I didn't agree with something he said the first time, but in reading again, I saw where he was coming from. I had the urge to write back to him, not even for him to see, but to simply get my thoughts out and share my perspective — no matter who agreed.

After I wrote a few letters in hopes to start a blog with the provisional title "Dear Hill," I hit a roadblock in my creativity. In writing back to Hill, I felt like I was stifling what I really wanted to say. It came off as cheesy. I could literally hear my friends laughing and feel them giving me the side eye. I can't even go back to read some of those letters because they are so cringe worthy. I felt like I embarrassed myself, to myself.

Growing up, my parents taught me how to use failure, or what can seem like failure, to learn and grow. I took my short-lived idea to respond back to Hill Harper and learned that I couldn't box myself in, especially when I write. I need to be able to speak my truth and stand on it. The blog had to be an open space for me to say what I want, and just be me and not feel judged.

My time at the newspaper publication really opened my eyes and showed me how valuable being in control of the narrative is. Prior to that internship, I think I knew certain newspapers and channels had their own agendas, but I'm not sure I understood how important it could be when those channels have the attention of millions. I wanted to create something where people from my environment could feel empowered by, and where people who weren't necessarily from my environment could get a clearer understanding. It was this idea that formed Urban X.

Urban X was originally going to be called "The Urban Experience". It started off around me wanting to just write about things I've been through in my life, and what I saw in my community. It was not my plan to bash or glorify anything; I just wanted to tell my story and give myself a creative outlet. However, after doing some thinking, my father and I decided that name was too long to type out in a URL and that title boxed us in to a certain format we'd have to follow if we wanted it to make sense.

During our brainstorming sessions, we thought about what the blog would be like in the long run. The Urban Experience as it stood alone is a very broad title that could mean anything, and *whose* experiences are we talking about?

I could simply only discuss mine, but then the blog would have to be named "My Urban Experience". Nothing wrong with that, but at the time I was only 21, and in my opinion, I don't think I have existed on the planet long enough to have a full interpretation on life in an urban environment, and life in general. Granted, I could talk about specific events and situations, but how in depth could I go if I don't bring them full circle with added perspective?

In my community reaching the age of 21 isn't a trifling feat, let me be clear, I just felt I would have been doing a disservice to readers by only writing about a portion of a long story. That wouldn't make me any better than the gatekeepers who control what the masses see.

My father and I talked about how my experiences growing up were different from his, different from my siblings, and different from my friends. These are all people I've spent considerable amounts of time with, but none of our life stories would be the same if we were to write them down on paper. They may be similar, but not exactly the same. It was a powerful revelation, so then we thought of calling the blog, "The Urban Unknown", because we all have stories and struggles that are unknown even to the people closest to us.

Aside from it being a corny title, Urban Unknown sounded like I would be writing short mystery stories or something. Besides, that one didn't really roll of the tongue too smoothly. Needless to say that one didn't last too long, but we felt we were on the right track.

The idea of being boxed into someone else's perception of us when we all have different paths to take was a concept we wanted to explore. We do have different experiences — even if we do live in the same community, or the same household. Our experiences are exclusive to us, and there the answer was right in our faces. We decided against a personal blog to only tell *my* story, but an entire platform where people could tell *theirs*. We looked at each other and said, "Bet let's call it Urban X."

Phonetically when we say the word "experience" the X sound is the most prevalent. Running with the idea that all of our experiences are different, and there is no way to know what someone's story or path really is, the X, like it does in algebra, will signify and stand for the unknown. It is the reason civil rights leader (and my namesake) Malcolm X changed his last name from Little to X. His teacher and mentor, Elijah Mohammad taught him that the last name given to his family wasn't truly his, and X was symbolic to him not knowing his actual family name.

The idea behind Urban X is that everyone's story matters, from the corporate CEO, to the schoolteacher, to the guy standing on the corner. Our triumphs and even our defeats ultimately shape us into who we are, and into who we are becoming; we can learn from them all. It is an open space for people to speak their truths, highlight their great work, and be in charge of their own narratives. We wanted Urban X to be a platform for anyone to share their ideas, expertise, and give in-depth analysis of the aspects that create the total "Urban X-perience."

The blog was created to dispel all myths, correct all falsehoods and misconceptions about our communities that were put in place by those who are not a part of them. I had grown tired of reading articles about my people that weren't written by my people, and it didn't necessarily mean Black and White. It is meant for people who were from my community.

We often read articles and biographies of great people, but rarely do we listen to the accounts of the people who are simply living and working towards more than what they have. As I am on my own personal journey, figuring out what works and what doesn't, I find myself constantly reading and learning about successful people who "made it" and as inspiring as these people may be, many times I feel like I can't relate. Society continuously showcases the finished product (the fame, the wealth, the accolades) never the process, as if it is not just as, or even more, important. In every neighborhood, you'll see all types of individuals with unique backgrounds that have lived lives that can fill pages in a book, and many of them are striving for something that will fulfill them and make them happy, why shouldn't they be highlighted? I want to hear from the people I can call my peers. Their journeys are just as important as the most accomplished individuals, and that is whom I want to hear from for a change. It became a mission to make this happen. The result is what you hold in your hands now.

As I previously stated, society and the media try to tell us what success means and what it should look like for everyone. We are fed images of famous entertainers, athletes, and multi-millionaires flaunting their wealth in exclusive events the average person could only dream about and are told this is what it means to be successful, to exude excellence. Within the urban community, there is a term often used that is aimed to highlight people that look like us, and is called, "Black Excellence." I believe this term is necessary because we should all be able to see positive images of our people. While I feel this is true, the idea that they are excellent because they have money can also be damaging to the people who are just trying to make it in their own ways, and in their own time. I feel it is imperative that we offer a plethora of other shining examples of what excellence can look like within our community. We should be able to create our own narrative of what it means to win and be successful, what it means to be an example of *Urban Xcellence.*

What is Urban Xcellence?

Similar to the idea that formed Urban X, Urban Xcellence derives from the idea that everyone's success doesn't look the same and doesn't need to. We are all working and striving towards something different, and while doing so, we should embrace everything about the community we come from; embracing our community as a gift and not a curse. It's knowing that the journey can be just as important as the end result. Urban Xcellence is being able to navigate the tough terrain that can be our environment, while still seeing the beauty of everything around you. It is a real grassroots movement.

Pressure can burst pipes, but it can also make diamonds; too often does history fail to tell the stories of those diamonds in the rough. Let's not make the same mistake and think the finished product is better than continuous growth.

Urban Xcellence is about the A-Y process before you get to Z, as my father would say. We all can't attend luxurious parties, or spend godly amounts of money on things, but we can ALL work to better ourselves and better the community around us.

Urban Xcellence is a never-ending lifestyle that everyone can be a part of, even if you don't necessarily live in an urban community. Xcellence isn't a fixed concept or stagnant idea. It moves as we do and adapts with the times.

Each week during the Urban X Podcast, my father and I find a story or two we feel exemplifies what we feel Urban Xcellence is. At first, we thought it would be a cool segment to mix in with our show. We had no idea that it would take on a life of its own. People began sending us inspiring stories from around the world and even emailing us their stories of their own personal victories. Our motto is, it doesn't matter what it is — if it's a win for you, we treat it as if it was a win for us.

Your 6-year-old niece just started her own lemonade stand? Great, we want to know about it.

You just got a promotion at work? Great, we want to shout you out.

Your son is going to college? Not only will we shout him out on the show, but we will also give you advice on what to expect.

We may all want different things out of life, but the feeling of having pride in something you accomplish, or the excitement in a new endeavor is something we can all agree on. That is an Xperience that is shared.

The idea for this book came about after conducting a series of one-on-one interviews with young men and women all on their own life journeys; many of whom I went to high school or college with. Through the use of social media, I was able to stay up to date with what they were doing, and they each agreed to do a sit-down interview on the Urban X YouTube channel.

While prepping for each individual interview, I thought of questions that the audience would want to know, but mainly questions I needed answers for to help in my own journey. I'm not sure they know, but their insight on work-life balance, dealing with the pressures of social media, and their determination has had a profound impact on how I attack my own work.

We conducted each interview at my father's home in the Bronx. Before my guest would arrive, we set up the lights, cameras, chairs, and the Urban X backdrop. My father and stepmother would ask me about the people I would be interviewing. My father would nod his head and tell me to put on a great show. He and my stepmother would be behind the camera as each person gave their story. After every interview wrapped, we all talked for a while about what they were planning (special surprises they didn't want to discuss on camera), and many of them commented on never being asked some of the questions I had for them. For some, Urban X had been their first on camera interview altogether.

It gets me excited that I am able to give my peers a platform to promote new projects they have coming out, or to talk about their businesses.

Once they left, my father would comment on how incredible all my peers were. I would proudly say, "Yeah, my friends are dope!"

I would say it not even really grasping the fact I knew some amazing individuals who are striving to hit their goals like I am. Even with the growing success of Urban X, I still had other aspirations that kept me up at night.

Not many people knew that since my senior year in college in the year 2015, I had a dream of writing a book and becoming an author. Growing up with the example my parents set, I was always an avid reader, and a strong writer. My father wrote his first book, *Hip-Hop Decoded* when I was in the sixth grade. In 2015, he released his second one, *Urban Culture Decoded*. He always speaks about his books being here long after he's gone and feeling proud he is leaving something behind of substance (other than his children of course). I wanted to do the same, but I always ran into the same wall. I struggled many times to get past an introduction, and when I did, I would hit a dead end later on in my writing. I could barely come up with a solid idea that I was able to articulate when one of my friends asked. Maybe I was too in my head, maybe I was self-sabotaging myself subconsciously. I don't know. What I do know is that without a solid concept, writing something longer than a standard essay would be excruciating.

One of my favorite authors, Ryan Holiday, spoke to this and said when people ask him if they should write a book, he'll flat out tell them no. This can sound harsh but he says if you have to ask if, you won't make it through to the other side to see your work completed. Writing a book because you may think it'll make you famous or a lot of money aren't strong enough reasons, you have to have something you *need* to say.

With knowing that, it was back to the drawing board for me. I knew me trying to force an idea would result in me putting something out for the sake of wanting "author" in my Twitter and Instagram bio.

So, I started to think about what I was passionate about and I came up with a few things: people, my community, and history. Again, there it was staring me in my face.

The *Insecure* show creator/actor, Issa Rae stated that aspiring entrepreneurs tend to feel the need to network up and try to make connections with established people, when networking *across* with your peers will help you and the other person. I took this philosophy to heart and began to reach out to everyone I saw making things happen in their life. If you were an entrepreneur, had a 9-5 job, or if you were positively affecting your community in some way, I wanted to know your story, and how you are striving to make history for yourself.

I love a good story. It's one of the reasons I studied history in college. To think that someone hundreds or thousands of years ago did something so incredible we're learning about it now was always an intriguing concept to me. Many times, these people did not have a reference point for what they were doing, but still managed to make some impact, small or large, that would ripple throughout time.

There is a Jay-Z line that I heard a while back that really resonated with me. He was featured on a Rick Ross song called, "Free Masons" and on that track he rapped about many of his personal struggles of trying to become successful in a confusing and unfair world. He said, "It's amazing that I made it through the maze that I was in, Lord forgive me I wouldn't have made it without sin." Music is subjective as we all know, but I interpreted that line as him being reflective on his life, and the different places his journey has taken him. The maze he mentions is the same maze we all find ourselves in at any given time. There are no instruction manuals to life, and we all have to figure things out as we go along.

I see Urban Xcellence as those day-to-day victories of being able to navigate the ocean that is your community. Yes, it is about highlighting good news — you got that job, you passed that exam, you started that business, and while that is beautiful, Urban Xcellence can be as simple as making it home safely after a day of doing those things.

My mother is a middle school teacher in the South Bronx, and she would always come home with stories about her students and what she saw them going through as their teacher. I remember one night, while I was still in high school, my older brother and I were having dinner with my mother and she told us about one of her students having a hard time. She pulled him to the side to see what was going on with him outside of school. My mother always expressed how important it was to know what children are going through because school could be the last thing on their minds if there is a problem at home. The boy told her that he gets jumped on his way home from school, and he has to always defend himself from people on his block. *How is a student supposed to be focused in class if he's worried about getting home after dismissal?*

After telling us about her student, she asked us what it's like to go home from school on a regular day. I think she was just asking about our daily routines, but she got more than she anticipated.

We recounted many days where we both had to defend ourselves, or even run from a dangerous situation just to make it on the train to get home. We talked about fights on the way to the train, on the train, and off of the train. We also talked about which blocks we knew not to walk through because we knew our neighborhoods didn't get along.

My mother looked frozen in disbelief; my brother and I actually laughed about it. She had no idea about some of the things we encountered just to get home from school, do homework or study for a test, just to do it all again the next day.

In the following pages, you will get to know some men and women I believe exemplify what Urban Xcellence means. Individuals who are in charge of their own story, and are in the process of doing some very special things in hopes of improving their own situation, as well as the people around them. Some are entrepreneurs, some are 9-5ers with side hustles, parents, and even disabled, but they all are hardworking. They're everyday men and women that anyone reading their stories can relate to and can see themselves in.

My goal isn't to define what Urban Xcellence is for you, but for you to read each story and create your own definition. The purpose of telling these "unfinished" stories is to show that there is beauty in the struggle. Each story will prove that every person's journey is unique and Xclusive to them, and that "Xcellence" is about perspective and has different meanings for everyone.

Just like the definition we created, none of these stories are fixed in place, they are moving along just as time does. They all still go through the peaks and valleys as we all do, but what's important is that no matter the size of the ripple; they are making their own history and finding their own happiness along the way.

Out of the Box

Inspired by Yvette Victoria

Stereotypes are an interesting concept. Don't get me wrong, I understand how detrimental they can be in the overall scope of society, but the way an idea can be formed about an entire group of people based on a narrative created by someone else is fascinating. Just think, when you walk past a person on the street, often times their mind is made up about you already; you don't have to say a word to them. In a few seconds they have a fixed image of where you're from, what you eat, how you talk, what type of music you listen to, and what they think your income level is. You may do it too, subconsciously, and not even realize it. In life, we don't have a choice in how others view us. It's not necessarily fair, but it is the reality. No matter what we say or do to convince someone, once his or her mind is made up there isn't much you can do. We may not have a say in what society thinks about us, but we do have a say in what we think about ourselves, that is all that matters, and that's exactly the mindset that drives Yvette Victoria.

Yvette is one of those people who refuses to be boxed in to anyone's perception of her. That mentality was also the driving force behind her annual Black History Month event that she holds in her community, Black History: Beyond the Box. There she highlights who she calls the overlooked or forgotten figures in Black and American history. It's a beautiful and unique concept, one that has shaped my intrigue with history in general. We usually picture the past as a straight timeline of notable people and events — here's what happened, here is where it happened, and this is the person who was responsible for it. Many times we unknowingly leave out the other links to the chain that creates these historic moments.

Yvette's dedication to showcase these stories was evident to me, as I recently attended the event. I saw the finished product, but like all great things, I also understand ideas such as this don't just happen. They come about through different experiences and later come into fruition whether you realize it or not.

Through the guidance of her loving family, she was taught to knock down societal barriers. Instead of asking why she couldn't do something, she asks, "Why not?" From a small town forty-five minutes outside Manhattan called Huntington, Long Island, Yvette described her community growing up as not being very diverse. "There were Black people in my town," she said, "but there wasn't many of us, and unfortunately it's caused people to have a warped perspective."

Yvette recalls many instances where she felt people wanted her to fit the narrative they had in their own minds. One of them was simply because she lived five minutes in the opposite direction of what was expected of someone who looked like her. If you've been from a certain place long enough, you know what the demographics of each surrounding area looks like. She gave a short break down of the neighboring towns and who lived there. "A lot of people that were wealthy lived in Cunnington Bay, Hanisha harbor, Lewitt harbor, or Coal Spring harbor and if you're black, people expected you to live in Huntington Station." Yvette is from Huntington, which is about a mile and a half away from Huntington Station.

The names can confuse anyone; I can actually see how easily someone could make that mistake if you aren't familiar with Suffolk County, or Long Island for that matter. However, Yvette understands that when people make that mistake, many times they are projecting their preconceived notions of what both areas look like onto her. "So people will ask me 'Oh, where do you live? Where are you from?' and I'll say, Huntington, and they'll reply, 'oh you're not from Huntington Station?' And I'm like, we don't *all* live in Huntington Station." She then added that Hunting Station isn't even a bad place to live.

Admittedly, Yvette grew up as a confident child. The support of her family created an environment that fostered self-love with a belief that there was absolutely nothing wrong with being Black. It's a mindset that she's proud of, and rightfully so. The harmful narratives that can plague the minds of other people have a way of injecting themselves into our own minds if we let them. If someone is told repeatedly that they aren't good enough, eventually they may start to believe it.

With a strong foundation and knowledge of self, Yvette was able to guide some of her peers who spewed ideas of self-hate. She explained that many young Black men and women in her community exhibited the very toxic mindset she was raised to combat. "Its [as if] white people are what they look to, what they inspire to be."

Yvette told me of an instance where she was trying to counsel a young Black girl who was having troubles while dating; she primarily dated white men. Yvette asked why she didn't try dating black men, and the young woman responded that she didn't want her children to have "nappy hair."

It's quite unfortunate when someone doesn't see the beauty in themselves, no matter what ethnicity they are. It can also feel like an uphill battle trying to convince someone who already has this perception ingrained. Yvette adds, "I was like, 'Girl, have you looked in the mirror? Do you know who you are? Everything about us is beautiful."

Interactions like this caused Yvette to really think about the people within her community. She could look around and see things that needed to change. Throughout our conversation, she referred to it as an ignorant bubble, one that she needed to burst because as it stood, there wasn't anything there feeding your greatness if you were a person of color.

The culture of Huntington needed to shift. What I found interesting was that although Yvette has larger aspirations to impact the world, she understands that she has to start with her immediate community.

When we hear the word "culture", thoughts of old paintings, famous monuments, and lengthy pieces of literature come to mind. While each can have a long and rich history, to limit what we understand as culture to something we can find in a textbook is shortsighted. There is a particular culture wherever you go and in whatever you do. Sports are a prime example of how the culture can be dictated on what and where it is taking place.

New York City basketball has its own language and customs all while following the rules and guidelines of the game. I can make the same comparison to Texas football and how children there are brought up and cultivated in a world where football is the dominant aspect of their youths; it is really a way of life, it is their culture.

After high school, Yvette attended the University of Bridgeport in Connecticut, where she majored in business administration. While there, she described feeling like she was losing herself as a result of having a poor semester. After her first year and realizing how expensive private college was, Yvette decided to transfer to SUNY Old Westbury because it checked off her personal wants in a school. It was close to home, it had a great business program, and she would be able to stay on campus. Once she was already transferred out of the University of Bridgeport, she received an email from them notifying her that she was on academic probation. It was at that moment she asked herself, "Who am I? Who am I becoming?"

Yvette grew up accustomed to success in the classroom. A self-described teacher's pet, she always served as a leader and example for her peers. She was known for receiving pride awards, thriving in honors classes, and being involved in student athletics and community outreach. After reading that email, she knew she was better than the effort she was putting forth. She wouldn't be on academic probation at her new school, but it served as a reminder. Her parents never pressured her about going to college, but she was raised on the idea that she could always do better. The mindset of not being put in a box started at home. "You can live out your God-given purpose regardless of whether you go to college, whether you go to high school or whether you get a Ph.D." She credits this philosophy with helping to ease the process of her becoming who she is today.

Growing up and idolizing Oprah Winfrey, Yvette always envisioned that her path would take her somewhere in business. "It's not by accident that many young black woman that are into writing, journalism, and communications or just any kind of production or entrepreneurship look up to Oprah like she's a conglomerate. She's a brand. She came from absolutely nothing, like if that's not a story that doesn't inspire everybody regardless of whether you're male, female, Black, White, Asian, I don't know what will. That's my girl. Like, my goal is to have her in my contacts in ten years. Like, we'll see if that happens."

Yvette entered college with a major in Business Administration, and a minor in Fashion Merchandising. Her goal was to develop and launch businesses, and sell them to investors. However, after transferring, she ended up graduating with a degree in Media and Communications. I asked why she decided to switch majors and her answer surprised me: "It really wasn't my choice, I asked for guidance from a particular advisor from the business department, and I guess based on what I said to him he thought media would be excellent for me. But I'm going to be honest, when I look back that's a bunch of garbage." I was taken aback by her response. While thinking back to the conversation, and her advisor's tone and attitude, Yvette told me that in retrospect she feels her advisor at the time saw her and thought Media and Communications would be "easy" for her.

It's a moment that she calls one of the greatest mistakes in her life because by switching majors and learning more about the field, she not only began to imagine herself in front of the camera, but behind it as well. She fell in love with the all of the possibilities it could bring. Initially, she thought maybe she could be a television host of some sort, like another Oprah. Now with more knowledge and expertise of the industry, she realized she was limiting herself and her thinking.

As we spoke, Yvette went on to mention documentary production as an area that has piqued her interest. Yvette explained that she saw it as a form of what she calls ARTivism. "Using art, using production to send a powerful message, to influence communities, to just change with this perspective on certain issues and topics, to expose, to bring awareness."

Activism and community building can come about in many different ways. We are all familiar with people hitting the streets with picket signs and holding public protests. While that was effective for a time, we now have to look at other avenues to spread our message. With the advent of social media platforms, one's message can be spread across the world with a click of a button.

At first, Yvette looked at her career opportunities and saw what was at the surface level, but by thinking outside of the box that was presented to her, she saw where she could use her strengths and bring value to her community. A powerful documentary can spark a great deal of change. It can cause people to ask questions, create conversations that can lead to new ideas. It is one of her many goals she hopes to accomplish.

Beyond the Box

Beyond the Box is the brainchild of Yvette and a friend. The idea came about after a discussion they were having in a coffee shop called Urban Coffee about the cultural atmosphere on Long Island. They talked about the self-hatred they both witnessed in their respective towns. We were like, "Oh my gosh, why don't these kids have any pride? Why don't they have any self-esteem? Why don't they know where they came from? Why don't they understand how excellent and how great they are?" From there they began to lay out ideas for an event that would keep the attention of the young people in their community.

I've been to enough Black History events where I can almost guess exactly who they would be highlighting and talking about. Martin Luther King, Jr., Malcolm X, Harriet Tubman, Frederick Douglass — the list can go on and on. Not that the aforementioned individuals aren't important and children definitely need to learn about them, but with school and mainstream media, talking about the same people gets old and tired. Trust me, those are for sure two nouns the youth stay far away from! So the task for Yvette and her partner was to think of a way to make Black history come alive. "Seldom do you hear about Marcus Garvey, Ida B. Wells, Annie Malone, or Black Wall Street. You don't hear about any of these dynamic stories that would inform the kids in our communities."

So where did the name "Beyond the Box" come from? I initially asked because I was genuinely curious of her creative process, but through talking with her I felt like I had a clear understanding before she even answered.

Every year in February, we are shown the same models for what is considered greatness in the Black community. Yvette and her team don't look to discredit any of these important figures, but to give you more information to add to the overall story. "I was like, okay let's do something where we're not talking about the people that we always hear about. That's where Black History Beyond the Box came about, and the name comes from take us out of the box. Don't marginalize us."

In school, social studies textbooks attempt to explain the African-American experience in half a chapter, often starting out by talking about our darkest period, slavery. My parents made sure I knew that although slavery was a crucial part of our history, in the grand scheme of things, it was a small piece of our past. I had the fortune of seeing and understanding what was taught through a different lens, many of my peers did not. Yvette spoke to this very notion, "we want them to know you did not come from slavery. It's not slavery, Abe Lincoln, Martin Luther King. That is not your history. We all have seeds of innovation in us, entrepreneurship. We were engineers, doctors; we were self-sufficient, self-sustaining. We are creative and we're resilient."

Hearing this made me think of my mother talking about when the limited series *Roots* first premiered on television and how her friends were in shock from seeing a show depicting Africans as free people before they were captured. When Alex Haley's *Roots* first debuted in 1977, it was revolutionary in it gave such a well-rounded nuanced story that many people had never seen or thought of. It didn't just come on at the point African's were on slave ships, but explained that it was a part of our history, not the entire one.

Bringing the Vision to Life

Like most ideas, Black History: Beyond the Box started with a pen and a notebook. It's something about writing your plans down that make it more like a reality than a wish. It becomes more than just a passing thought that you will forget as soon as you get a text or refresh your Twitter feed. Writing your plans on a piece of paper can seem like an arbitrary action, but when you think about all the people you admire and what they've accomplished, you can feel better knowing some time ago their starting point was similar to yours. No matter what social class they were born in, they decided to put their ideas on paper. Yvette explained why this step is so important no matter what you are trying to accomplish. "It makes it more real. You brought something that came from the soul realm, your internal realm, your mind and now you're bringing it into a tangible realm. On a piece of paper, in a notebook, on a poster, I don't care — write it out. Whatever that idea is, whatever you thought about back in second grade that somebody told you was stupid — write it. Get it out your mind and see if you'll look at it a little bit different like, 'you know I think that I might be able to do that'."

The next step was tackling the actual logistics to pulling this event off. Yvette began to utilize the skills she picked up over the years from community building classes and outreach programs she has been involved in. That meant making calls to local non-profit organizations to partner with them, to ask for donations, or to inquire about using their space for the event. It was imperative that Yvette and her team worked to cut the cost down and not spend too much of their own money. To do this, they had to think of creative ways to use their resources to make it happen because Yvette wasn't going to let anything hold her back from bringing her vision to life.

As she spoke about the process of getting the event off of the ground, I could sense a tenacious will power that we read about when we study the greats. She joked that she would go as far as to have the event in her living room if that's what it took to accomplish her mission.

After making calls to local organizations, Yvette and her team were able to solidify a space for their first program at the Spirit of Huntington Art Centre. Throughout her life, Yvette has observed her community and vowed to make an impact that would alter the mindsets and expectations of the people within it. The first event being in her town is a testament to that goal. She didn't forget where she came from and why she wanted to put this event on in the first place.

Yvette and her team understood that because there are so many forgotten figures when Black history is discussed, there is no way to cover all of them in one event, so when they began planning, they started with a specific industry.

The objective of the event is to show examples of Black people thriving in different areas, and why you can, too. The importance of representation cannot be understated; to see people who look like you thrive doing something you would have never thought possible could do wonders for the self-esteem. By showing different career paths we can take, it opens the world even further than once thought possible for someone who had a limited vision of where their life can go.

Imagine how free the "nerdy" child must feel when he or she realizes we don't all have to be athletes and entertainers to be successful. While it's a constant fight to convince other people to take you out of the box, there is also a battle within yourself to do the same. Beyond the Box is looking to bridge that gap of what we always see, and what we can be. "We start by looking up people we don't often hear about. Who's not on the radar? Who's not a part of a narrative in Black history?"

The first year of Black History: Beyond the Box, the industry that was explored was Africans and African Americans in cinematography and photography. There were about 45 to 50 guests in attendance. It was definitely an accomplishment to gather that many people to listen to presentations about figures they had never heard about. It was also a learning experience for her because it was the first event. Obstacles are inevitable. However, it's how you look at them that determines if you are made for what you are trying to accomplish. Someone impatient may have seen the 50 people and been discouraged at the turnout. Not Yvette! She even joked that all of the chairs they rented were in use, so she was happy.

The great thing about throwing a yearly event is you always have something to strive for the next time. Like an athlete training in the off-season, you can always find something to improve that will further what you are trying to accomplish.

I was able to be present at one of the Beyond the Box events, and I was blown away. The industry chosen to explore when I attended was African American entrepreneurs and trailblazers. It was held at the African American Museum of Nassau County. Prior to reading the flyer, I had no idea such a place existed. Yvette explained that she specifically chose places that no one really goes to or appreciates. This can cause people to want to learn more about the museum or community center, and possibly attend on their own. That is another way of bridging the cultural gap in your community.

Yvette and her team were able to almost double the amount of people that came to the first Beyond the Box event, thus growing the brand even more. There I was able to hear about men and women who strived to better themselves and their communities in a time of immense uncertainty for people of their pigment. There was absolutely no way someone could leave that place and not feel inspired, but also humbled.

To think, a woman like Annie Malone, who was born to slaves, was able to build businesses, generate millions of dollars, and give back to her community at a time when she couldn't go on YouTube and watch an inspiring video from Gary Vee. To do the things she did as a Black woman back then is nothing short of amazing. I had never heard of her before going to Beyond the Box and was floored when I learned she mentored Madam C. J. Walker, who is always discussed when February rolls around. Learning about Annie Malone was a perfect example who why this event is necessary. Why did history forget her? And why with all the information at our fingertips (literally) do we not actively try to become our own gatekeepers? Black History: Beyond the Box is working to answer those questions.

After her most recent event, Yvette was asked the same question that is presented to all high achievers: what's next? She told me she definitely wants to take Beyond the Box global so she can aid in changing bias, but she knows that she has to start from the ground up. "We have a greater vision for that cultural imprint that we want to make on Long Island, not just the Black community. We are diversely segregated on Long Island and we want to bring cultural awareness."

Yvette understands real change comes when people are brave enough to do something about it. From an early age, she had been frustrated with the labels placed on her by society, and also with the people in her community who accepted them. She had the desire to make an impact and do something very difficult, and that is to change perceptions.

Every one of her experiences has prepared her for this mission, and I for one, can't wait to see what she does next.

The Power of Persistence

Inspired by Dorian Drummond

Each of us have the choice of whether or not to let negative experiences affect how we live our lives going forward. When life deals us an undesirable hand, we have the innate choice to let those adverse circumstances tear us down, or build us up. We all grow up and go through experiences that shape us into the person we are becoming. And although it may be difficult, we have to constantly reaffirm our vision of what we want our story to be. If we allow our sight to be clouded, we will only see where we've been and never see where we can go. The next example of Urban Xcellence is a person who is continuously fighting to beat the odds and overcome every obstacle placed in front of him, Dorian Deshawn Drummond.

When I began brainstorming people that I could ask to be a part of this book, Dorian was the first person that came to mind. He is one of those people you always want to see win because you understand where they came from. Very down to earth and humble, but an inspiration to anyone who hears his story because it exemplifies one of the most important aspects of Urban Xcellence — relentless perseverance.

Dorian came into the world with the odds already stacked against him. He was born with cocaine in his system. Directly from the hospital, he and his siblings were taken away from his birth mother and placed in foster care as a result. From the day he was born until the age of five, Dorian, along with his older brother and sister were moved around from house to house, family to family, due to them not being wanted. And in some cases, they were abused by the people tasked with looking after their wellbeing.

During the first five years of his life, Dorian just wanted somewhere he could call home. He wanted to be around people where he could be himself. "When you think about home, you think about peace, you think about love, you think about comfort. We didn't really have that growing up. We were bouncing around a lot, trying to get closer with a mother figure, because that's what I really wanted was just love, structure and affection. Sometimes, we'd be in one house and see a stranger at the door and say, 'Hey, this is your new parent,' and we'd just move to another house. It was just like that."

It's easy to take for granted some of the most basic essentials we need to survive. Health, loving parents, and a stable home were all not a given in Dorian's life during some of the most important years in a child's development. He had to learn very early that life isn't always fair.

As he sat in front of me telling his story, I couldn't help but think of the other children who grew up as he did but were not able to pull themselves out from under the overwhelming weight the world had place onto them.

Prior to our conversation, I didn't know much about the foster care system. I guess you could call it the ignorance of privilege, but I couldn't even tell you the difference between foster care and adoptive care. I always thought it was the same thing, but I now understand it isn't.

Dorian explained that foster care is seen as a more temporary situation where care givers, (commonly known as foster parents) are paid a weekly allowance to take care of the child until they come of age or are adopted. The child's legal parents can also have a say in important decisions about the child's wellbeing. Adoption is more of a permanent situation where the adoptive parents get legal custody of the child and can give the child their surname. Adoptive parents are given some financial assistance early on, but that eventually stops.

Dorian believes many people become foster parents solely for the paycheck and not because they want anything to do with the children, many don't even like children. Dorian's future plans consist of adopting to help change a child's life. He sees it as a way of paying it forward. He wants to be able to provide a home for a child in need in order to prevent them from going through the same things he and his siblings did.

While he doesn't remember everything that went on during his time in the foster care system, his brother, who's five years older than is, has a more vivid memory of what happened to them as they were moved from house to house. "He told me that he used to get beatings anytime I had an accident in my diaper, he had to take care of me. He was tormented, he still has a really bad burn mark on his hand."

At the age of five, Dorian and his two older siblings were adopted. He remembers the moment of being in a foster home and his would-be parents, the Drummonds, walked through the door. He was told that he and his siblings would be going home with them and that was it. Dorian now had parents. "It was a huge blessing; it was the first time we were wanted."

I found it interesting his parents adopted all three of them. Even with the limited knowledge I had on adoption, I knew many parents go in with the mindset of only adopting one child, maybe two, but three? I saw it as a very noble act as Dorian and his siblings could have easily been separated, and he almost was. His mother really only planned on adopting Dorian's two older siblings and not him. Dorian was very sickly as a child. Along with being born with cocaine in his system, he also had a heart murmur, and asthma. Leading up to the day they went to their new home, his mom wasn't sure he'd make it and she didn't want to live with the possibility of losing a child. Luckily his mom decided to take in Dorian as well, and he has since grown up healthy.

Now, the story doesn't end with Dorian and his two siblings living happily ever after with their new parents, they still faced new challenges. At the time they were adopted, the Drummond's were in their fifties already. His mother had children of her own from a previous marriage, but his father didn't and that was their main driving force for adoption in the first place. The next year they adopted another child, and two more in 2001. Now the total of children in the home is six. But it didn't stop there. As I previously mentioned, his mother had children of her own. She eventually took in her two grandsons as well – now that's eight kids.

Eight children, all living together and bringing with them different struggles and experiences. In hindsight, Dorian can see how his living environment would be tougher than most of his peers. He also saw how his parents struggled to keep all of his siblings together as a family unit.

Dorian mentioned that he absolutely wants to adopt, but he said he would only want to adopt one child because he has seen firsthand how difficult it can be to take in more than one child. I can't fault him because only he would understand the trials and tribulations that can come with a situation such as his.

Like a lot of young boys, Dorian dreamed of going to the NBA, but his parents weren't able to invest in any extra help to get him to perform at a higher level. He explained, "So when I wanted to join a travel team they'd say 'no that's too far,' or if I wanted to do basketball training they would tell me, 'no that's too much money.' So everything I kind of had to do or learn on my own." He joked that backyard basketball is only going to do but so much.

College Bound

Living with so many different personalities took a toll on Dorian during his high school years, and by the time he was applying for college, he wanted to get as far away as he could. "I kind of wanted to get away from New York; I wanted to spread my wings. When you're growing up living with ten people, eventually you want to break through." He went on a free HBCU (Historically Black College and University) college tour where he was able to visit and see different schools outside of New York. He even applied and was accepted to a few but wasn't able to attend due to the high cost of tuition. He learned what it meant to apply to college as an out-of-state student. He didn't have a lot of financial aid to cover the expenses necessary, like tuition, room and board, and textbooks. Let down by this, he explained that he'd given up on going to college altogether. If it weren't for his guidance counselor he would not have gone at all. He told her his situation. She made some calls and helped him get into SUNY Old Westbury's EOP program at the last minute. EOP stands for "Educational Opportunity Program" and it provides access, as well as academic support and financial aid to students who may not have otherwise been accepted to that college.

In college, Dorian was able to find that sense of independence he was looking for growing up. Old Westbury wasn't too far away from where he lived with his family in Brentwood, Long Island, but living on campus he was able to learn more about himself while staying true to who he was no matter what people thought about it. "I feel like only people close to me kind of knew who I was. But outside looking in, a lot of people had thoughts or went by what they heard or what they thought about me because the whole persona I had. They saw a kid that didn't like to party, doesn't like to have a good time — and that wasn't the case. What people don't understand is my life wasn't the same as an average college kid."

During his freshman year, Dorian was a full-time student and he worked two jobs. His parents were both elderly and were going through health issues at that time. Mom had multiple sclerosis, and dad had Alzheimer's, so he did not want to bother them if he didn't need to. He made sure he found time to go back home and check up on them in between going to class and going to work. "I had to learn to be responsible at a very young age. There were times I wanted to party, but I'm like I have to work in the morning. I didn't have the ability or luxury of saying I'm going to hit mom and dad up to transfer money into my account, I didn't have that."

As he said this, I felt myself getting smaller in my seat. Sometimes you can listen to someone else's struggles and immediately feel humbled. I'm not one to compare issues, but all I could say was "wow" as I listened. I wondered if I could've completed my undergraduate degree when faced with the same obstacles in my way. I had a few jobs while going to school and I still was able to ask my parents for money. I was fortunate to have a safety net that Dorian didn't have.

I officially met Dorian at the end of second semester of my sophomore year. I say officially because we both were in the same African American Studies class together, but I didn't even know he was there until the last week. He sat in the back, barely raised his hand and rarely spoke. He would come to class, give in his work, and when it was time to leave, he did so — there was no lingering around afterwards. We joke about it all the time because we can each think back to instances when we needed help with a difficult assignment and could have used each other's help. However, that semester I could see how people could have certain perceptions of Dorian. Although he was well known and liked on campus, he kept a small group of friends whom he trusted and rarely partied. Even after he joined his fraternity, Alpha Phi Alpha, his character never changed. When you think of college fraternities you may think of wild parties, but Dorian wasn't like that before and he wouldn't let letters change him now. People expected him to be seen at more campus events or around more women, but he understood his fraternity stood for more than that and made sure he never strayed too far from what made him uniquely him. "The history that organization has from Martin Luther King Jr., WEB Dubois, and Jesse Owens — it was so much more. I just feel like it represented me. And, you know, how I carry myself, and the image I kind of want to have. I didn't need to become an Alpha to have the ability to get women or go to parties. I already had that ability. I didn't care about that."

Truth Hurts

There were many aspects about "normal" college life Dorian found very trivial. Not because he thought he was better than anyone else, but because he had other concerns that weighed on his mind heavily —one was finding his birth mother. All of his life he can remember wanting to know who she was. His adoptive parents wouldn't even show him his birth certificate until he turned 18. Dorian isn't sure of the specific reason, but he can recall feeling angry, like they were hiding something from him. He just wanted to know something about her, a name, where she was from, nationality, something. He was so in the dark that until he was 13 he thought one of his foster parents was his biological mother. It was frustrating not knowing his full story; not even being able to put a face to the person because he was so young when he was taken from her, but he waited until his 18th birthday to get one piece to the puzzle. "It was a very emotional day. I found out what hospital I was born in. I was born in Brookdale Medical Center, and that's when I found out my mother's name and the address she lived at when she had me." It was a moment that Dorian waited years for. He was able to uncover the mystery of who he was. He was born Deshawn Dorean Roberts, on July 15th, 1993 at 5:45am. Due to the drugs in his system, he only weighed three pounds. When Dorian was adopted, his parents wanted to give him a fresh start in life so they changed his name. First they changed the spelling of his middle name, and then they switched his first and middle name.

Now that Dorian had some information, he set his sights on trying to find her. During his sophomore year in college, he and his girlfriend at the time went to an address that was listed on his birth certificate to see if there was a possibility his birth mother still lived there. They both went to every door in the apartment complex and slid notes under each door with his name, his story and contact information with the hopes someone would get back to him, but they came up short. In the years that followed, he tried many different angles to find his biological mother, but to no avail. All he could do was hold on to the hope that one day he would find her. Even when it seemed like a lost cause, deep down he had to tell himself it would all work out. He told me that this process taught him that everything happens on God's timing.

Personal journeys aren't that personal when you have people in your corner who care about you. As Dorian is on his mission to find his birth mother, I wondered how his adoptive parents felt about it because although they didn't physically give birth to him, they raised Dorian to be the man he is today. He told me that his father was happy for him, but he was mainly concerned about his mother's feelings. Dorian explained that she would periodically check up on him to see how his search was going but he understood how this area could be sensitive to her. "My mom tried to tell me that she was supportive, and she doesn't mind, but you know how moms are, and I know my mom. I know she was kind of scared, and worried that she was going to be replaced and forgotten. I made sure to tell her 'you are my mother, that's my bio mom, you don't have anything to worry about'." Dorian understood that family ties go far beyond blood relations; his life up to that point has shown him that your family are those you are in your corner and have your best interest at heart. The Drummonds weren't blood, but they were his parents.

Although he had many setbacks in his pursuit to find his birth mother, Dorian never quit. He may have slowed down because life can take you in different directions, but he understood what we at Urban X have come to understand — the journey is just as important as the destination. It had been years since Dorian first saw his birth certificate and learned his mother's name. He completed college with a degree in Media and Communications, the first in his family to do so. He went the entire summer jobless after he graduated. He worked at Applebee's waiting tables and delivering food to cars waiting outside. Then after his shift, he would work as a janitor at a local gym. He did this six days a week.

Speaking from experience, after you graduate from college you expect to have some time to get your life together before you are forced to really become an adult. I was twenty-one when I graduated from school, legally allowed to drink, and considered an adult in society's eyes - but I still didn't think I was ready to go out on my own. Dorian felt the same way but was soon put in a position where he had to sink or swim. In November of 2016, his mother sat him and his siblings down to discuss something that would shake the foundation of their family. His parents planned on moving to Connecticut at the end of the upcoming year. His mother wanted to make sure all eight siblings would be prepared to be on their own. The news hit them all hard. Dorian, in particular wasn't expecting to move out for another year or two. He was just starting to structure his life post-grad. He was making decent money, just got a new car, began paying school loans back, had a great credit score but now he was forced to move his timetable up a bit. Then on December 2, 2016, his mother approached them again. The timeframe for everyone to move had once again changed. Instead of his parents moving at the end of the next year, they would be leaving at the end of the month after Christmas. Dorian's heart dropped. His mind was spinning as he went through a bevy of emotions. "I felt abandoned. I'm hurt. I'm angry." He told me that he felt under the circumstances in which he grew up, that he felt he did everything that was asked of him, he stayed out of trouble, he completed college, and now it felt as if he was being punished.

Through time and many conversations with his mother, Dorian realized he wasn't being punished. I think he knew that as everything was happening, but his emotions were causing him to think differently. It is very understandable. His anger was then placed to his siblings because he felt they weren't doing their part to help their elderly parents. Although he doesn't blame anyone now, he understands why his anger was misplaced — he was scared. He had no idea what he was about to do. His mother even offered him the opportunity to stay in the house he was raised in with a few of his siblings, but he decided to go out on his own after really considering his options. He made the decision to live out of his car. He admits that it probably wasn't the smartest idea. Everyone around him called him hardheaded but he felt this move was best for him. He still went to work, he showered at the gym he worked at, and often times slept there, too.

He did that for about a month until his former high school guidance counselor found out what his living situation was. He offered Dorian a place to live at his mother's basement apartment. "I got lucky. When I was trying to search for apartments, I was told I needed about two months of rent, security deposit, not everything included. I'm like oh, this is hard, this is a lot for a twenty-three-year-old." However, that month taught Dorian a valuable lesson about sticking to his gut feeling. He knew staying at his old house would not have been the best situation for him. Yes it was a roof over his head, and yes it would have been much better than living in his car, but he was thinking long term. Dorian would've been paying most of the rent and taking on most of the responsibility. It was not what was best for him. He credits that situation with adding to who he is becoming today, just another part of his story, and more proof that he can overcome anything placed in front of him. In a way, he grew from being in an uncomfortable position.

Outside from a few people, everyone around Dorian was in the dark about what he was going through. He didn't tell anyone that he was basically homeless and needed help. He revealed this fact at his housewarming for his new apartment. I was shocked when he told us, and also angry with myself, too. It was because I remembered hanging out with him and not being able to see any signs that anything was wrong. He kept a smile on his face like he always does and carried on like it was a normal day. When it got late, he simply gave everyone a dap and left. During the housewarming, I pulled Dorian to the side to tell him that he should never feel like he couldn't tell us things and that we would more than gladly help. He responded that it was something that he just needed to do.

True Tenacity

The housewarming felt like a victory lap for Dorian. He proved people wrong about whether or not he would be able to overcome; some of those naysayers were in his own family. He just used their voices as motivation and found a way, but something was still missing. Throughout everything that was happening around him, he never forgot about finding his birth mother. His focus may have temporarily changed, but the idea she was out there still sat with him every day.

After most of the people left from the housewarming, one of Dorian's friends stayed behind. After a few drinks, his friend told Dorian about how he found his own father using Facebook. It wasn't like Dorian never tried this method before. It was one of the first things he did when he first got her name from his birth certificate, but nothing came up. His friend convinced him to try again. Dorian typed her name in the search bar and many people with the same name appeared. He wouldn't have to search through each profile, because only one woman with the correct name was Black; he was getting warmer. It felt as if the stars in the Universe were aligned because as he was going through this woman's profile everything seemed to fit. He still needed to match up another crucial piece of information to ensure that this woman he's looking at on a Facebook page is indeed his birth mother. What was ironic was that when he finally got his birth certificate, he discovered that his mother's birthday was actually the day before his on July 14th. As he was scrolling down the Facebook profile, he thought if he went down far enough, he would see birthday wishes from other people and he did. "So then I was like alright, let me do the math, because if she's turning fifty-six then it has to be her. I did the math on when she had me, and she was thirty-four. So if she's fifty-six then it has be her. I did the math and I dropped my phone and ran upstairs. I was in tears."

He didn't have to give it much thought. Dorian went back on Facebook after everyone had left and direct messaged this woman who he believed to be his birth mother. Dorian told her he was born as Deshawn Dorean Roberts at the Brookdale Medical Center, and followed that up with a simple, yet powerful question: "are you my mother?" He woke up the next morning to a message that said. "Hey, I'm your mom, here's my number, call me right now." In that one moment, his life changed.

I asked Dorian what fuels him to keep going. He told me that his story, along with his long-term vision is what drives him to be better, to overcome. Since graduating from college, Dorian admits his aspirations have changed from simply wanting to be on television to wanting to make a positive impact on the lives of others, mainly children and young people. He understands a story like his can show others that they can make it through the most difficult circumstances and find their way to the other side of it.

Every day he's building a personal brand that he feels one day will leave a major impact on the lives of others. Dorian now goes by "Mr. Drummond" as an ode to his father. "My dad, he was like our Superman, there was nothing he couldn't do. He was our taxi man, our handy man, anything we asked."

Currently, Dorian is teaming up with his former high school to do talks in the auditorium, poem days, and is trying to be the next commencement speaker at the graduation. He is also starting his own motivational radio talk show in which he aims to inspire and teach people how to go through personal struggles, stay motivated, and find purpose.

So what does success mean to Mr. Drummond? To him it means living a full life on your own terms. He acknowledges the feeling personal achievement can bring about, but thinks living a happy life is a greater barometer of true success. "Some people maybe want to be rich and have wealth, and some people are fine with the 9 to 5. It all depends on your terms, but I think to be, to live happy, and to get through life you have to try to take the positive out of every situation and understand why it's happening. To be happy, man, everybody wants happiness."

Walking Pass The Doubt

Inspired by Elijah Bowser

It can be very easy to take some aspects of your life for granted. We begin to almost expect things without stopping to think about all of the people who either don't have, or can't do what we do. We become so lost in our everyday minutia that it's rare that we stop and just be grateful for being able to go to work and provide for our families, come home to a loving environment, or simply walk down the street. The next person I sat down with has been a constant reminder in my life that we all should be grateful of what can be perceived to be the "little things." My younger brother, Elijah Bowser, has always been able to see life differently from the average person because he had to. Diagnosed with Cerebral Palsy at the age of two, he has been unable to walk, and has used some sort of aid to get around for the majority of his life. However, in spite of what can seem negative, he has strived to prove to everyone around him that his disability *is* his ability.

In the midst of me reaching out to friends and old classmates for this book, and thinking about who else fit the ideal mold of Urban Xcellence, I had another one of those "in your face" moments as I was helping set up for another week of Elijah's podcast, the WATE (World According To Eli). After setting up his banner, and fixing the lights, I watched him use his surroundings to get to his seat, make sure his glasses were clean, put his headphones on and proceed to put on a great show for his audience (and spank my father in a debate). I was instantly captured by how far he had come from being born so small that it seemed like he could fit in one hand.

The episode lasted for about an hour, in which he talked about the latest NFL standings, his favorite basketball games from the week, and the movie he went to see the night before. If I didn't know him and simply just listened to his podcast, or watched the video on YouTube, I would not know this kid is unable to walk. How can I talk about this concept of Urban Xcellence, and making a way for yourself no matter what when I am ignoring a shining example right in front of me?

Listening to him speak in his show and give his own perspective to the week's hottest topics reminded me of the original idea of my blog Urban X. We all have different experiences that shape who we are. Although Elijah and I are siblings, and were raised together, his experience as a disabled child completely differs from mine. I knew I would be doing this book a disservice by not including him. I was also curious to see what new information I could learn about him. Even though I was present for many of the big moments in his life, I know I had no real clue into his thinking and how he preserved what was going on.

When I first sat down with Elijah, I asked him what it was like growing up, "interesting and unique," are the two words he used when describing his childhood. Born two full months prematurely, he had a multitude of health issues in the first few months of his life. Due to him being born at three pounds and fifteen ounces, he had to spend about four weeks at the hospital's newborn intensive care unit (NICU). Then about two months later, Elijah was infected with Group B Meningitis, which he could have died from. "I had a bad cry, and my mom knew it immediately, and she was like, dude, we have to take him to the hospital right now." When they got to the hospital, his mother's concerns weren't taken seriously as they were not attended to for over twelve hours. If it weren't for one particular doctor, Elijah would've died. "My [parents] tell me the story all the time. Dr. Amy came in to check on me, and she told them that they were going to keep me overnight. Then around 8pm as she was about to clock out, she came back to my parents to check on me and noticed my skull was really swollen." The doctor jumped right into action because she knew if something wasn't done quickly, that this baby wouldn't have much of a chance. By my stepmother's account, the doctor literally took over the hospital, moved things around herself, screamed at people, and made sure Elijah was properly taken care of. However, because the hospital took so long to give the proper care, there may have been some lasting effects that resulted in Elijah getting brain damage. Group B meningitis has a list of side effects, many of which affect the brain directly. After he was put on medication, Elijah was discharged and able to come home. "My parents were just happy to have their son, you know?"

Everything seemed normal until his parents began to notice he was developing slower than other children his age. At the age of two, Elijah was still getting around by crawling on the ground instead of walking; this prompted a visit to an organization called United Cerebral Palsy. There, specialists had him complete exercises like matching shapes in the correct holes and when he wasn't able to do so, along with other similar cognitive exercises, the examiner explained that he did in fact have Cerebral Palsy. Funny enough, he said that his upbringing was pretty normal in spite of the circumstances. "My childhood was pretty cool you know? I'm simple; I played with my toys, watched cartoons and watched sports with my dad. And my family treated me completely normal; nothing was different. If I did something wrong, I was disciplined right away." He went on to talk about growing up with his siblings. "It was cool, because on one hand I had two big [brothers] with you and Marcus, who were going off to college and working jobs. I could always see you guys at least once a week to say what's up and try to beat you guys in video games." I can say firsthand my older brother and I, along with my younger sister, didn't cut Elijah any slack. We treated him like he was a normal kid. We play fought, joked together, got in trouble and I think Elijah appreciates us for it.

Even though we as his family did all we could to treat Elijah like we would any other child, it was only a matter of time until he wanted to physically do what other children did. He has a sister who is two years younger than him who began standing and walking while he was still crawling. I can't imagine the physiological toll that can take on a child to see his younger sibling literally run circles around him and he can barely stand. I remember attending a younger child's birthday party and watching all of the kids run and have fun while Elijah tried to follow them. He crawled so fast but was always at the back of the pack. Still he kept a big smile on his face.

He also started to take a special interest in sports from watching games on television and playing video games like Madden NFL or NBA 2K. Naturally, he wanted to do the things he saw himself. "I remember, in particular, dad was taking you to football practice, and you had your helmet and shoulder pads on and I was like, 'um mom why can't I wear equipment like that?'" His mother had to sit with him and explain that he had a disability that limited what he could do. I'm sure the way my family treated him did amazing things for his self-confidence, but there was also the reality that he did require extra help and attention. This brought about a weird dynamic for his parents because right behind Elijah they had another child who did not have a special disability and wasn't really old enough to understand the situation.

Our younger sister, Odyssey, was your typical little sister growing up. She was super annoying, very opinionated, and loved to bother her big brothers. Even though she could physically do more than Elijah could, she still saw him as her older brother and always questioned why he got what she called "special treatment." She often brought her issues to my father or her mother directly. "There'd be times where she got upset like, 'why are they giving him extra help with homework or giving him extra attention?' and I would try to explain to her that I wished I could do some of the things she was beginning to do. My parents were already teaching her how to get on the bus by herself." I had to seriously pause when he said that. I even stumbled on my next question because it was another aspect of life I never thought about and took for granted. Being able to just get on a bus and go somewhere on his own wasn't something he could just do, but he saw everyone around him being able to experience something he couldn't.

Up until this point in our discussion, I pretty much knew what to expect. I literally watched him grow up and I was front row for many of his experiences in the home. I was always a little nervous of how the outside world would treat him. While he was out he used a wheelchair to get around. I was worried people would judge him or underestimate how intelligent he really is because he was in a wheelchair. That may have been my own insecurities because how I've looked at individuals in wheelchairs in the past. Living with Elijah taught me otherwise, of course.

Although I lived with my younger brother for a short period, there were still experiences he had that I had no idea about. Learning more about him was what I most looked forward to when he agreed to help me with this project. I got a chance to learn about his experience in school. I know kids can be cruel, so I was shocked to hear that aside from one or two isolated incidents his peers treated him well. "My classmates were all very nice and respectful, but they were curious, they just wanted to know why I was in a wheelchair and I never got offended by that at all." The kids in his class would simply just ask him what happened and he would explain what cerebral palsy is and how it affected his brain and leg muscles.

Many of his classmates, and even some of his teachers were surprised at how articulate Elijah was as a child. My guess is that they saw a disabled kid and already had him labeled. "They'd be like, 'wow he can talk, he can do all of these things' and then they kind of just treated me like a regular person." He reiterated that he never took it personal, but more as a challenge to change people's perception of him and prove that although he made be limited physically, he can still use his mind as well as anyone else. He admitted that he never really much cared for school because he often found himself to be bored with the entire experience. Waking up early, getting on an unreliable school bus with a long commute, and sitting in one place listening to his teacher go on and on about information he deemed unimportant. That didn't mean he didn't do well. Elijah is so competitive that even if he did not like the subject he tried his best to pass the class. He hated to fail. Now that he is older, he can look back and understand that the structured school environment just wasn't for him. He learned and processed information a bit differently, and he knows that it is okay. There are plenty of adults who go their whole lives hating school and feel there might be something wrong with them, when that might not be the case.

WATE

To foster Elijah's passion for sports, his parents had to get creative. If he were able to walk and run, they would have been able to put him on a local youth team for whatever sport he chose to play, but since that wasn't the case, they had to think outside the box. They noticed how well he remembered player's stats, and analyzed games and wondered if he'd be able to hold his own in a debate. My father would challenge Elijah on the most current sports story, and they both would go toe to toe. For someone who has always had developmental issues, I have always been impressed with how sharp Elijah is. He took his frustrations that he was unable to actually play and focused that energy into really learning about each sport. He was able to tell me who had the most RBIs in baseball, who had the highest QB rating in football, and who had the best shooting percentage in basketball without stuttering. He could watch a football game and tell my father what coverage the defense was in before they snapped the ball, and he could guess who each week's winners will be based on statistical data. This special talent birthed the WATE, which stands for the World According to Eli.

At first, my dad wanted to do an entire ESPN First Take style show for Elijah since at the time it was his favorite show. I would come home from school and he'd be arguing with the television like the reporters could hear him. Naturally, my father thought a YouTube show would be perfect, so we ran a test show. That didn't work out too well. Elijah looked flustered with all of the cameras and lights, directions from us while still being able to give his analysis; it just wasn't the right fit. "I really wasn't feeling it, like the big bright lights, and reading Teleprompters, and like because I'm a little bit slower to process information it would kind of be a drag to try to do all of that and do my thing." He was obviously a little discouraged after the test show and vowed that he'd do better. While no one doubted him, we just wanted him to be completely comfortable.

One day while watching ESPN, Elijah noticed one of his favorite shows was actually a radio show that the network filmed. He stated that if he wasn't worrying about the cameras he would be more comfortable and he would be able to work. He then brought it to my father's attention that they should do an online radio show because he liked the low-key feel. After much convincing, my father decided that he and Elijah would do a father and son podcast together and just put the footage on YouTube. They also tweaked the idea of what the show would be as well. Although Elijah loves sports, he is also very well rounded in what he consumed. The World According to Eli would be about what he saw, what he cared about, and his take on life from his own perception. Music, sports, video games, and culture pretty much encapsulated everything Elijah is about. He would be able to showcase his unique voice and opinion on a bunch of topics and be free to just be him. During the first few episodes he did not even mention that he was disabled; he wanted his work to speak for him, not his physical ability.

He hopes to be able to use his growing platform to empower other disabled people to follow their own dreams, whatever they may be. It's a message that falls right in line of what Urban Xcellence means.

Gaining Independence

Aside from his podcast, he has had a silent motivation that only the people closest to him know about, and that is to gain his independence. For years, Elijah got around either crawling on the floor at home, or using a walker, or getting pushed around in a wheel chair. I remember getting a call my senior year in high school from my father, and he told me that while getting ready to leave for school, Elijah decided he no longer wanted to use his wheelchair. It was a huge deal because he came to that decision all on his own when he was still in elementary school. He explained that after seeing some of his friends graduate from using wheelchairs, to walkers, to crutches, and some don't even use anything to help them walk, he felt motivated to get on their level. He just showed up without his wheelchair and shocked all of the school staff. First, because it was a bold move from a shy kid, and second because he actually needed permission from the school to not use his wheelchair. "I was just a little kid. I just thought, you know, I could just show up to school without it." After some bargaining with his school aids, Elijah was allowed to attend school without his wheelchair. Getting around with a walker tested his stamina and his upper body strength, but he understood from watching his peers that he needed to practice and he would become more efficient.

As Elijah got older, having his independence became extremely important. "I was like eventually, I need to try to live in this big world on my own, without any help. No guidance, no calling my parents like 'oh I'm lost.' I need to know my directions and my surroundings." This need to experience independence caused Elijah to become more daring in his life. At dinner one night, he told us about the time he used his walker to cross the street on his own because his friend was able to convince Elijah that it was simple. We were all shocked and concerned. While we encourage him to find his independence and do things on his own, we also want him to be safe. But he assured the family that he took the proper precautions. Another example of him just going for it was on his 18th birthday. I got a text message from his mom that said, "here is Eli's gift to us" and two videos followed. I was initially confused because why would he be giving any of us a gift on his birthday, but I shrugged it off and watched the videos. What I saw didn't register right away. I saw Elijah walking without assistance across the living room and back the other way. I looked closer at the video trying to figure out what was holding him up, and to my surprise, nothing was holding him up! My boy was walking!

I couldn't believe what I was seeing. I got emotional because I had gotten comfortable with the thought that he may never walk on his own, and once again Elijah proved me wrong. I'm glad he did. I called everyone and even posted the video to my Instagram page because I was so happy and proud. I called Elijah so excited and he was just so cool and calm about it like he had done it before. He told me he'd been practicing while no one was around and wanted to just go for it so everyone could see. "I was turning 18, and I was like, okay, I'm going to try to make it to my room without touching anything. If I fall screw it, I can get back up and do it over again in two weeks, and just keep trying you know?"

What made the moment even cooler was that he didn't even announce he was about to get up and walk — he just did it. His mom was in the kitchen not looking, and my sister was sitting nearby looking at her phone. She said she just looked up and from the corner of her eyes saw Elijah walking on his own. She too took a moment to process what she had just saw. Once she realized her mind wasn't playing tricks on her she screamed, "Mom Eli just walked!" His mom played along and said, "oh cool", but my sister could tell by her nonchalant response she truly didn't believe it. Elijah then took the opportunity to show off and walk back to her. His mom lost it, rightfully so.

He told me that walking on his own wasn't really for anyone other than himself. He too had never thought about what his life would be like if he never had cerebral palsy, "Someone from my high school [asked me] 'dude what happens if you wake up one day and just are able to walk by yourself?' I'm like, honestly, I don't know." He went on to explain that because he was born with cerebral palsy, he didn't have the blueprint on how to properly do it. He was starting fresh.

Disabled Is Abled

Today, Elijah is working to be able to walk completely on his own for long periods of time. He now uses arm crutches to get around, but in the process, he is getting his legs stronger. He has hopes that soon he'll only need to use one, then soon, none at all. As he works every day to find his independence, he has also set his sights on an even grander goal. Starting his own podcast and walking on his own are what he deems as personal successes, but he now wants to uplift other people who are like him. He has taken the first steps to start a not-for-profit foundation for other high functioning disabled children/teens called, Disabled Is Abled. He wants to help people with disabilities be able to live on their own, help their families pay for college tuition, and the other many expenses that come along with it if they choose to go. The idea came about because his best friend got accepted to a college and needed some help to pay for everything. I know firsthand that being on a college campus on your own is the ultimate independence and as much as he wants it for himself, he also thinks about others. "That's like a big fear for all of us, not all disabled kids can move freely. Some are stuck in a motorized chair, and I'm pretty sure they have dreams of doing their own thing, live by themselves."

I find it admirable that he wants to do so much for a community that society tends to ignore. He knows that although the hand he was dealt may not have been ideal, he can still do what he can to help the lives of others. In a weird way his disability helped him see the world around him with a more unique lens. He also joked that his disability helps him skip the lines at amusement parks and airports. Elijah hopes that his story, along with his mission to help other disabled people, will inspire all types of people to do what they can to effectively change the world for the better.

Every day he works out, he thinks back to when his teachers and aids would tell his parents to just keep him in a wheelchair because he would never be able to do anything more than that. He doesn't harbor any ill feelings towards them, he just uses the doubt as fuel to get better and show people who he really is. "I don't see it as like, a personal thing, or like hold a grudge against them, [it's like] they're judging a book by its cover and once they read the book they know, okay this is a dope book."

Truss Your Process

Inspired by Andre Truss

I often brag about my group of friends — whether it's to other people, or on my podcast. I will never miss an opportunity to let the world know that the team I have around me is top notch. Not only because of the amazing things they are doing, but also because we hold each other accountable and make sure that we reach our goals after we set them. The next example of Urban Xcellence is one of my closest friends, Andre Truss, who at the time of me writing this has a forced me to agree that if I don't complete this book by the date we set, I owe him $500. And if I do finish in time, all I get is the satisfaction of finishing.

I met Andre on the first day of freshman football try-outs in the ninth grade. Off of my first impression, I thought him to be a loud, arrogant know-it-all, and a bit of a coach's pet. He would jump up to be the first in every drill, talk trash to everyone, and always told the coaches what they wanted to hear. I wasn't entirely sure if I liked him very much to be honest.

One day, a few of the guys from the team and I were roaming around the school and Andre saw a piano and sat down to play. *Of course he thinks he can play this, just like he thinks he can do everything else,* I thought. To my surprise, he was actually very talented on the piano. I was taken aback, and slightly ashamed of myself because I had judged him before I ever really gotten to know him.

I had Andre in my mind as one way based off of my perception. Once he was done playing, I told him that he was very good and asked what made him take lessons. His response that day resonated more than I think he knows. He told me, "My mother put me in a lot of extracurricular activities to keep me busy." Being from the Bronx, it can be very easy to stumble in the many pitfalls that come along with being from a tough environment. My mother made sure she signed my brother and I up for everything just so our time always had purpose. Whether it was karate, football, basketball, piano lessons, summer camps — she made sure we were busy. It was at that moment Andre and I began to click.

Born in Jamaica, Andre arrived to America at a very young age, and his family settled down in the Soundview section of the Bronx. He told me that even as a kid he knew he wanted more for himself. Andre often felt out of place in his neighborhood because of everything that went on — the drugs, the fights, and the gangs. He told me that he felt like an outsider, he went on to explain, "My mindset was always on making it out of the environment from a young age versus what other kids were thinking about. I felt like I was a little bit isolated or I felt like a loner." He had a vision of his future, and it wasn't in Soundview.

I would describe Andre as a jack-of-all-trades. He played on both football and basketball teams, was on the academic honor roll every marking period, played an instrument, rapped and recorded his own music out of his room, and ran a side hustle selling candy in school. I was a loyal customer. I asked him about everything he was involved in; I wanted to know what drove him and his answer was simple: he wanted to get out. He knew he might not go pro in football or basketball, but he understood his hard work would take him further than his current situation. "I had three plans in my mind. It was either I was going to get out by just sheer hustle, I was going to get out by basketball, or I was going to get out by the mixture of hustling and basketball. That's all I had, but in my mind, I never really had any dreams of going pro or doing anything like that. That was never really an option for me." Typically young guys from urban communities see sports or music as their only viable options for success, Andre saw each as a stepping stool that would help him obtain his overall goals.

Even though he didn't have dreams to go pro, sports definitely played a major role in his life. He first began playing soccer when he lived in Jamaica, then when he got to America, his mother purchased him a basketball. After countless hours of practice and games in his local park, Andre became known around his neighborhood as the young kid that could flat out ball. He even got the attention of mentors who encouraged him to take basketball more seriously while training him to get even more skillful. His natural athletic ability allowed him to cross over and play other sports like football. He was so physically gifted that during try-outs I initially didn't even know that it was his first time playing organized football, that is, until we put on pads and began tackling (that's another story). I remember freshman year asking him what made him join the team and he shrugged his shoulders and said, "I wanted to see if I could." Now that I think about it, it was on the field we forged a tight friendship. I believe sports reveal character, rather than build it, and through his hard work he became one of the team captains, along with yours truly.

Along with sports, Andre had another passion — music. In high school, any time someone made a beat on the desk or lunch table, Truss (as we called him) was right there with a quick freestyle full of witty punch lines and wordplay that made us all scrunch up our faces as if we just all smelled something foul. "Part of me is always going to be a rapper. It's an expressive form. I never wanted to rap because I wanted to be famous. I wanted to rap because that's how I expressed my pain. It was how I put into words what I was going through in my life that I felt like I couldn't go talk to somebody about." During our senior year, one of our classmates was murdered. Truss took that pain and recorded a song that shared the sentiments we were all feeling. The song was even played at our friend's wake.

So where did this love for music and rapping come from? He watched someone close to him rap all the time about what he saw around him, and it inspired Andre to do the same. Only catch was Andre kept that talent to himself. It wasn't until his friend approached him and basically challenged him to quit being afraid and to just rap about what was in his heart. Andre admitted to me that he felt disrespected at first because of how he was approached by his friend, but after a few moments he understood the message that he was trying to send. "He was like, 'Yo, stop being a kid. Man, I feel like you got a lot of talent. You being afraid of letting people hear you is stopping you from actually putting out good music to the world.' That was something I appreciated from him." From that moment, Andre never looked back. He started to carry a notebook everywhere he went so if an idea came to his mind or he thought of a dope line he would write it down immediately. Knowing how Andre is now, it was hard for me to believe that he was ever nervous about showing anyone his talent.

Destined for Greatness

If you hang around Andre long enough you will get used to his big talk and infectious attitude. He always seems to be thinking of a new business venture, a new deal to be a part of in some way and he literally plans everything down to the last letter. When I met him, I did not have any business of my own or entrepreneurial aspirations. Andre however, seemed to be destined for it. "I grew up in the sense of always having a business mentality. My parents have photos of me with my little suit and briefcase. I started businesses when I was young. Doing like pencil businesses. Water, selling water. Doing all the New York hustles, but I was always very business oriented." One of the people he credits this to, is his adoptive father. When Andre turned sixteen, his mother made a conscious decision to allow him to be taken in by a family that was able to take care of him financially. "I looked up to [my dad] a lot. He was very driven, straightforward, and charismatic. He controlled the house. He was a man to me."

Andre's adoptive family was white and lived on Long Island, a stark contrast to what he was accustomed to. He had a prior relationship with his new family because both his adoptive mother and father were previously his teachers in elementary school. He explained that he's always felt comfortable around them. Then he told me it was tough because of how the outside world received him *with* them. "This is a guy that's been teaching me how to play chess since I was in second grade. His wife taught me how to write." Although Andre gives credit to his adoptive family, he makes it clear that his birth mother was the one to lay the foundation of who he is. He hates when people attempt to discredit who he is because of how he looks compared to how his adoptive family looks. He has had experiences where after speaking with someone, then telling him that a white family took him in, they would say something like, "oh that's why he speaks so well." When in actuality it was his mother who laid the building blocks for Andre. "My mom was actually very hard on me. Before I even met them I was actually really good at school. They just enhanced it because they had more opportunities than my mom had." What Andre's mother did by allowing another family to take him in must have taken a lot of courage to put aside any reservations she may have had. She saw and understood that her son had an opportunity to walk through some new doors that she, as well as Andre, would have never known about, to no fault of her own by the way.

Although Andre isn't biracial, I saw his position as unique because he is a Black man in America, who's from the hood, and who clearly has white people in his life who truly care about him. I wanted to know what kind of conversations they had about race relations when an incident happens. He explained to me that they never shy away from the discussion, they attack it head on and his father explained very early that he was entitled to feel any way he wanted. However, it is because he's spent so much time around different cultures that he feels he is able to step back from situations and try to make sense of them with a little more nuance. After all, he knows his adoptive parents would do anything for him and some of his closest friends from the naval academy are white and he knows he would be able to call them for anything if he needed. For Andre, knowing that just re-establishes his belief that people aren't born with hate in their hearts, "you adapt for different thoughts over time."

Driven

If you were to visit Andre's office today, you would find a bunch of books with sticky notes coming out of them, legal pads filled with client information, and a white board with what looks like scribble in different marker colors that document future plans. He's a visual thinker. He can't simply say he wants to do something; he needs to map it out step by step for it to feel real to him.

When he was in high school, Andre mapped out a plan that he thought would bypass college and put him on a fast track to success. He had the grades to attend any college he wanted, but instead he ended up going to the United States Naval Academy. For me, and the rest of our friend group, it seemed to come out of nowhere. But as we talked, I realized it came about from a failed chess move.

During his senior year of high school, Andre had an unofficial internship on Wall Street with a financial service firm where he was able to contribute to the team he was working with. Truss explained that he did so well that the man who owned the firm eventually noticed him. So he thought that he would continue to work hard, build a relationship with the owner then propose that he start working for the company full time and skip college. Well, that didn't go over well. They had their meeting as planned, and in true Andre Truss fashion, he attempted to sell himself and show why he would be an asset to the company. "I'm being the salesman of a lifetime to him. I'm like, 'Hey, instead of me going four, five years in college, why not groom me for four to five years. Think about how much money I'm going to make the company and make you.' He just laughed at me [and said], "No chance in hell." Andre immediately got upset because it wasn't the response he was expecting. On paper it made sense. Instead of him going to school to get this job, or one like it, work with the skills he has now and he can make the company more money. Right? Wrong. The man saw all of Andre's hard work and recognized his potential, but he still wanted him to go to school to get a quality education. It just so happened that he was an alumnus of the Naval Academy and thought the school would be a great fit for Andre, so he set up an entry interview for him.

Sounds like a great opportunity, but the problem was Andre did not want to go to college at all. He purposely didn't apply for any schools in spite the fact that he had the grades, internships, and the extracurricular activities. He was dead set on having things go the way he wanted. "I didn't tell my dad. I had all the letters and all the stuff like that, but I never actually filled out any of the applications. I was just pretending to fill them out, in hopes that I could buy enough time to actually get my way." Andre grew up playing the game of chess, he understood making his plans become reality would take moves and countermoves, so his next idea was to completely butcher the interview for the Naval Academy. That way he'd have no choice but to figure things out on his own.

The Dean of Students was the person who conducted his interview, and at first everything went along pretty standard. He asked him questions about himself, his grades, and the sports he played in high school; all typical interview questions. For the last question the Dean asked Andre why he should let him into his school. Andre saw this question as the perfect chance to mess things up and responded in the most arrogant way possible. "I was like, "Honestly sir, I don't need your school," he continued, "I'm smart. I'm diversified. I can literally do whatever I want. It's either you're going to let me into your school and I'm going to be successful by way of the United States Naval Academy or you're not going to let me into your school, and I'm just going to grind for five years, and still be successful off my own name. Now the ball is in your court, but I know I can figure out my way." My mouth dropped as he was telling the story. It seemed to be something out of a movie scene. I'm sure it must have felt great in the moment to do what you want, but as an adult now, the first thing I thought about was the man who got him the interview in the first place. What did he think about Andre's stunt? "He was in the back, just lost it. He's panicking because once again, as I'm learning more about networking, he put his name on the line for me. I didn't understand that at that time, but that was a very disrespectful thing for me to do." Well his planned backfired because the Dean of Students liked his answer so much that he offered him admission to the Naval Academy on the spot.

At the Naval Academy, Andre had a bit of a culture shock. He told me that his experience there was tough, but also fulfilling because it was the first time being in an environment where he did not have to worry about his safety. His responsibility was to be the best student he could be. He did admit that mentally it was a challenge for him. "We have a motto at the school. It's like, 'The worst place in the world to be at but the best place in the world to be from'." He would play basketball every morning. Swim practice Tuesday and Thursday in the mornings because Andre did not know how to swim and I guess it goes without saying that knowing how to swim in the Naval is a must. Then the basketball team would go look at plays. From plays they would have breakfast. He was doing more than most people do in their entire days all before 8:00. After he ate, he had class from 7:00 to 11:00. Lunch from 11:00 to 1:00. Then back in class from 1:00 to 4:00. Once all his classes were done, Andre was back in basketball practice from 4:00 to about 8:00. He also had many military obligations he and his classmates would have to do. After all of that, he had a load of homework that had to be completed for the next day.

Andre summed everything about his time in the Naval Academy up in two words, "it sucked." For four years he had to endure an environment that demanded the best out of him and did not take excuses. He had to be mentally and physically fit at all times and it could weigh heavily on a person if they don't embrace it. After a while, Andre saw the beauty in the process. Everything that has come after doesn't seem so scary because he's been through enough in the Bronx, and in the Naval Academy. He told me about some of the lectures he attended by very influential people, and people he now knows because of his connection with the school. Charles Bolden, for example, was the first African American to be at the head of NASA and is an alumnus of the Naval Academy, and also happens to be a member of the Omega Psi Phi Fraternity, which Andre is a part of as well.

Something that I learned from Andre during our talk was that everyone from the Naval Academy is required to join one of the military branches upon graduation, it's called commissioning. As of right now Andre is still an active duty Marine Corp officer stationed on Jacksonville, North Carolina. It's a long way from the Bronx and Andre has grown up so much from the kid who was just trying to get his way. Prior to him going to the Naval Academy, then on to the Marines, he was a focused and driven individual. I feel now that he has overcome the hurdles that came along during those same obstacles, have only amplified who he is.

He's always wanted to be that person out in front to lead his team and he feels the Marine Corp has helped him see what it's like to be "tossed in the fire," as Andre put it. As a Second Lieutenant, Andre is required to make important decisions all the time, be able to stand on them and take responsibility. "Anybody that knows me is like I always harp on 'make a decision, make a decision, make a decision,' because that's what was beat into my mind." In the military, Andre is learning very important leadership skills that he has transferred over to his business dealings.

Businessman

Recently, Andre and his business partner opened up their first real estate brokerage firm in Jacksonville, North Carolina called "Tellers Truss Realty." If you visit their website, on the first page it says that their goal is to "transform your expectations about buying or selling a home." That expectation is what drove Andre's motivation to delve into the field of real estate in the first place. Originally, he wanted to buy a home with a mortgage loan that is guaranteed by the United States Department of Veteran Affairs, or a VA Loan. He wanted to put a roommate in the house so they could pay half the mortgage then he could pay the remaining half. Over time as the money his roommate pays, Andre would make in equity. His plan was to make a couple extra hundred dollars a month, the only problem was the first real estate agent Andre worked with did not live up to the standards that he was used to as a military man. He had no information on a property Andre was interested in, had no answers to any questions he had, and was all around incompetent. He took so long to draw up a contract that another person swooped in a bought the house Andre wanted. That experience forced Andre to wonder if he could do a better job by himself.

As Andre spoke to other people within his unit about his experience, he met someone who had a similar story of dealing with agents who were incompetent. Unbeknownst to Andre, he would become his business partner. "He came to my unit, he was real sharp. Just really on the ball. I felt like we ended up creating a company out of frustration for the agents that we worked with." Real Estate, like many other types of businesses, follow the same power structure, and that is what attracted Andre so much to it. His passion for business never waned as a result of being in the military, so it would make sense that he would use his leadership tools and his overall discipline to want to create a business of his own. After dealing with the first agent who couldn't answer any of his questions Andre thought, "How could this man make a living without the proper systems in place?" Once he and his business partner had their minds set on actually starting a business, they knew that having a system was a step they could not miss.

As we were doing the interview, I paused to change the camera batteries and he immediately went to answer an email and take a quick call. When we resumed, he continued to talk about the systems that need to be in place for a business to thrive. "I'm not even in Jacksonville, North Carolina and I have six people that's ready on standby right now if I were to ever get a hot call. It's just the way that I function."

It was a proud moment for me when Andre sent pictures of his new brokerage firm to our group chat. We knew how hard he worked for this moment and how long it took, but what was important was Andre did not skip a step and he did not try to cheat the process, he embraced it.

The day of his grand opening, I watched and re-watched all of his videos on Instagram and Facebook because I knew this "overnight success," as some of our peers saw it, was really a culmination of three years of sleepless nights and countless hours of planning, researching, and negotiating. It has been dope to witness someone use any resource they had available to them to grow, make mistakes along the way, and create something for themselves. That is what Urban Xcellence is all about.

Boss Up!

Inspired by Anna Okolo

Have you ever gone into a business, or looked around at your own job and thought you could do it better? We all go throughout our days with amazing ideas that never end up being much more than that, ideas. Imagine if we actually put them to work and attempted to make those vague concepts into tangible products, or businesses. It was that feeling of, "I'll do it myself" that inspired my next example of Urban Xcellence, Anna Okolo to start her own business and become her own boss.

Anna holds many titles. She is the CEO of her company, Boss Basics Marketing, co-founder and CEO of Style and Grace Event Productions, and she is also the events manager for a hit YouTube show called BK Chat. The path she is currently on looks much different than what was expected of her growing up. As a young Nigerian woman, Anna saw her career prospects as very limited and quite frankly, she resented everyone for it. She began getting into the habit of proving the people around her wrong and creating her own lane. Anna explained to me that within her culture, there are some expectations of her because she is a woman. "They have this expectation that you get a good job, then you can go home, and you can take care of your children and your husband, and they expected you to be married by twenty-five and have kids by twenty-eight and all this stuff." She almost went her entire high school career following this idea that was pre-set for her before she realized she had her own passions. As she thought back on her teenage years, Anna laughed because everyone around her just knew she would either be a teacher or nurse; she didn't want to do either.

Around the age of fifteen, Anna joined an afterschool organization called FBLA, the Future Business Leaders of America. FBLA is the largest career student business organization in the world and as a member, Anna realized that she had a real passion for business and public speaking. Being a member of FBLA, Anna was able to compete against other students locally, regionally, and nationwide in academic competitions like impromptu speaking. She fondly recalls winning fourth place in the nation, and in doing so convincing her parents that she was not destined to be a schoolteacher or a nurse. "My parents were there, we went to Florida, and they gave us our own suite and everything. I remember I was competing against all these different people and my dad was shocked. He was like, 'wow I didn't know that you could do all of this'." Anna wanted to be in some type of business, but she for sure wasn't in the business of limiting herself for anyone.

Born in Nigeria, Anna's family immigrated to the United States by way of a Visa lottery. During her earlier years, Anna explained to me that her living environment was not the most stable because her family moved around a bit before settling on Long Island around the age of thirteen. They started in Brooklyn, and then ended up in Queens.

Then Anna spent three years at a boarding school in her homeland Nigeria. When she returned, she often times felt out of place, culturally speaking. When I asked her about her parents, she told me flat out that they were very strict. As a result, it was very difficult for Anna to forge friendships with many of her peers in school because their interactions had to cease at 3pm because she would have to go straight home. If she didn't go directly home after school then that meant she was in her AP class or SAT prep, or she was preparing for the U.S. citizens exam. Anna understands how the social structure of high school is. If you weren't doing all the usual things all the other teens were doing, you might be considered a nerd or weird, and on top to that, she was from another country with a thick Nigerian accent. Her social life was not best to say the least and at the time she harbored bitter feelings towards her parents for it. "It was not until like recently that I understood why my parents were strict. They were shielding me because a lot of these kids nowadays, they do crazy stuff and ended up in crazy situations, and your parents are just trying to protect you from that. But when we're young, we don't see it as that. I just saw it as my parents just don't want me to live life. They don't want me to enjoy life."

For college, Anna attended SUNY Old Westbury. There, she took the opportunity to figure out what she was good at, and where she could use her strengths, hone the skills she did have, and pursue her passions. She initially started off in accounting and finance, then after some soul searching, she came to the realization that she wasn't too fond of math. She ended up getting her Bachelor's degree in Politics, Economics, and Law because along with business, Anna did have a love for politics as well. However, while she was in college, Anna began to push herself to learn more about marketing and management. Her goal was to become more knowledgeable so once she graduated she could combine all of her skills and work in positions that would need her expertise.

No Role Models

Any time I sit down with someone, one of the first questions I ask myself, and then I ask the person is "whom was their role model growing up." Depending on the person's upbringing, their role model could be someone who was very present in their life or a celebrity they've actually never met but still inspired by what they do. When I asked Anna this question I was taken aback by her answer. She told me in a very plain, matter of fact tone, "nobody." She went on to explain that she saw everyone as no better than her so in modeling herself after another (flawed) person would be like diminishing her own value and greatness. "Like, I never really had one growing up because I always looked at people and thought, why am I looking up to you? Like, in my opinion, unless you're God or Jesus, you're not perfect." I thought it was interesting how she differentiated what a role model and what a mentor was in her mind. She felt a role model is someone who is perfect in everything they do and say, whereas a mentor is someone you can take individual qualities to add to how you want to run your business. With mentors, Anna takes everything with a grain of salt. "I look at my mentors like, it's literally how they have their business, their organizational skills, and how they network with others, what it is that they're doing to obtain success in the most ethical and moral of ways." It was the first time that I found someone who shared my feelings on having a role model.

I was in the third grade when my father made me read the Autobiography of Malcolm X and I remember getting to the part when Malcolm found out some disturbing information about his spiritual leader, Elijah Muhammad, and how it totally crushed him. It was like a part of him died. My father took the opportunity to explain to me that no person is better than me and all humans are bound to mess up sometime. This lesson was reinforced when one of my teachers in high school randomly stated to the class "don't get too close to your idols, you might be disappointed." I'm always inspired by some of the things people accomplish, but I will never see that person for more than what they are, a human being. I think Anna would agree. "I feel like when I look at somebody and be like, I'm going to be like that person, I'm kind of taking away from my own capabilities."

Working in a corporate environment can be difficult by itself. Being a woman in that type of environment brings about another set of challenges as well, and Anna wasn't shy about speaking on the many different obstacles she has faced as a woman in business, and how it inspired her to start something for herself. "It's been horrible. I'm not even going to lie."

When Anna graduated from college, she began working for the Boy Scouts of America. She was a District Executive where she helped with events and managing certain accounts for the company. She was the only black woman, and the only woman that was a part of the executives. At times when trying to voice her opinion, Anna felt as though she was speaking to herself. The Boy Scouts of America, she explained, were very conservative in their approach to many issues and Anna was attempting to be a new fresh voice, but she found many of her attempts to be for nothing.

Level Up

After her time with the Boy Scouts, Anna thought she would have a better opportunity to create change within an organization if she worked with start-ups. She found a new job in New York City and decided that she would work so hard and diligently that the founders would have to recognize her. Anna was waking up at five in the morning, getting to work by 6:30, and not leaving until 8:00 PM at night. "[I was] working my ass off to prove to them that this is me, this is what I do, and I'm bomb at it." She did so well that she actually got a promotion to become the company's Digital Marketing Manager.

It was Anna's job to understand the company's needs from a technological perspective. "So the way a lot of companies are set up now, they are only focused on the physical manifestation, which is basically you go to events, meet and greets. Hey, here's my business card, I do hair, or I do makeup, or I sell clothes, come work with me or come support me and then that's it."

Anna's job was to go further in how she connected with potential customers or partners. "We do email automation where we understand the type of people that are your clients. Then we do social media branding. And through social media, you understand the type of followers you have, the type of things they're looking for, the target audience that you have. She also was responsible for knowing when the perfect time to post certain pictures was or which hash tags that her company should use to affiliate with each post.

Using social media for business purposes is so much more than posting a picture and hoping someone sees it and likes it. Anna had to understand analytics and Search Engine Optimization (SEO) so her company's business page would show up on Google's first tab instead of on the tenth page.

I could tell by how knowledgeable Anna was that she was passionate about what she was doing. She had a strong confidence that she could go into any job and handle her business, and that is what she did. Sometime after she was promoted, Anna was tasked with putting together a holiday party for the company. And like all things she sets her mind to, Anna went above and beyond. The party had aerialist, disco balls, and a packed dance floor. It turned out to be the most successful event the company had ever thrown up to that point in December 2015.

Two days later, Anna was laid off.

Although it was a tough moment for Anna to deal with, it was then that she learned a valuable lesson in business and in corporate America: no matter who you are, or what you have done for that business, if they need to let you go, then you will be let go.

Something interesting Anna did notice was that most of the people who were let go from the company happened to be women and minorities. Could be something, could be nothing, but she made sure to take a mental note. "[I feel like] most companies, only hire females, especially Black women, to fill in the aesthetics where they want to look diverse. They want to say, 'hey, we're a diverse company. We have this, we have that, so don't speak negatively on us. Let's get more investments. Let's get more sponsorships."

However, when she looks deeper into these organizations, she finds that the Black women present are relegated to answering emails and typing memos when they are more than qualified for high positions.

From that situation, Anna got another job for a higher position making more money, but she soon ran into the same problems of being ignored. It was like speaking to brick walls, she explained. Her ideas would go ignored no matter how much sense they made. She told me of a situation that took her over the edge and was the springboard for her starting her own business, Boss Basics.

Anna made a marketing pitch that she thought would grab and retain new clients, she wanted to personalize the campaign, so people felt more connected to what they were buying into. She wanted to understand each person's personality and market based off of those qualities. *Is the person an introvert, a dominant person? What is their role at work, what are they really like?*

One of the executives wanted to stick to the old way of just grabbing everybody's email names, sending one letterhead and just sending it away. While Anna was trying to have a constructive discussion about her idea and why it would be a good idea to at least try, the executive dismissed her and in front of the CEO and COO by telling Anna to shut up. "I was sitting down there, and I was in front of my desk, and I was just like, no, no, no. No way!"

Later, the company happened to be going through cutbacks and letting people go, they offered Anna a severance package or a demotion — she didn't think twice about the decision and took the check.

It was with that money Anna began to lay the groundwork for her own business, Boss Basics. Since graduating and having many experiences where she felt she wasn't being valued because she was a woman, and talking with many of her friends who were having the same experiences as well, Anna felt if you can't beat them, join them. Not join their team, but join their field and compete with those very same organizations that worked to hold her, and many of her contemporaries, back.

Bossing Up

While working at many of these places, Anna acted as a sponge, soaking up information and different skill sets that would help her along her own journey. What makes her qualified to help other businesses with their digital marketing? Well, she's done so for multiple companies she's been employed at. She thought, why not use the same capabilities she has acquired through her studies and work experience, but instead of her employees taking her ideas and making money out of them, then have that money trickle it down where she only got a small percentage of it, she could use her ideas and get a big bulk of the money. She knew that she would feel much better knowing that these are her ideas and instead of her waking up at five in the morning to work for somebody that doesn't necessarily care about her, she would be waking up in the morning to better herself, her brand, and her business.

As of right now, Boss Basics is a team of one, but she uses technology to her advantage so she isn't overwhelmed. Anna schedules postings for her clients. If her clients go to events, she lays out a game plan for them, so they just aren't present, but they make their presence felt. She makes sure her clients consider how to look at these events and how to affiliate yourself with other people at these events.

With Boss Basics, Anna also makes sure that her clients are keeping up with their own clients through emails, "…just making sure that their popularity, they're following, their pay and everything is as consistent and as clean as possible." Anna understands how important social media can be to a person's income if they have a product or service they sell. The more people know you through social media, the more money you can potentially make.

Now, Anna isn't naïve to think all you need is 100,000 followers and you'll be rich. She further explained that it's what you do or who was following you through your social media that determines the type of money that you make. "So that's where my role comes in to help people really understand that and making sure that they get the most bang for their buck."

Two Is Better Than One

At Boss Basics, Anna is the sole proprietor. She has to make every decision, good or bad. At her other company, Style and Grace Designs, Anna is the CEO, but a co-founder. She has a business partner who's title is the COO. It is a much different structure than Boss Basics because she is working with someone else who has a different way of doing things.

After Anna put on that event for her old job, she realized that she did in fact enjoy that whole process. Also, as a Nigerian woman, in her culture she attends many events and parties every year, so it was natural that she'd want to create a business centered on events.

Anna linked up with one of her classmates from college, another Black woman named Jade, who put on events for people while we were in school like birthday parties or baby showers and Anna would think, *how the hell did she do this by herself?*

One day they were talking, and Anna just came out and said, "Yo', let's start a business," and Jade agreed. The name Style and Grace Designs comes from their respective personalities and roles within the company. "[Jade] brings the style and I bring the grace. We started doing events for our friends and we started posting it on social media. Then she started focusing more on the events and I started creating the web page, making sure the social media was together and then we started bringing everything together." Anna and Grace hope to expand Style and Grace Designs, and bring their signature look to events everywhere.

Inspired to Thrive

As our interview went on, I could just tell Anna had a special drive for business and entrepreneurship. I wanted to know where it came from because neither one of her parents own a business and her older brother was more into his studies growing up, he is a doctor. When I asked what happen for her to birth this type of hustle, she gave credit to many different positive factors growing up, but she also gave credit to a negative one — the death of one of our college classmates, and a great friend. She noted how ambitious he was, how driven he was, and loved by everyone. His tragic death sparked something in her that she wanted to leave a legacy for herself and her family for generations to come.

Speaking for myself, when I got the news of his passing, I felt so stuck. He was an all-around cool guy to know, warm spirit, inviting personality, and he was incredibly *humble*. It was the first word anyone could think of as they got up to share warm memories of him. I have always found that quality to be the most elusive when dealing with people. This was obvious by the fact there was only standing room at one point of his memorial service.

As I looked into the sad faces, I began to think about the fact we were all brought there at this very moment because of one person who decided human life could be disposed of at their whim. Then I began to think about why his death affected me in a way I couldn't explain, and then the answer came as I looked at the rest of my college family.

Many of the people I went to school with all have great minds and great ambitions, it was just so unfortunate that our communities that build us up and provide so much inspiration can be the very thing that take us away. It was a reality that I'm sure many people not from urban communities don't have to face. One of my friends put it best, "Other people graduate college and go back to their safe neighborhoods; we graduate and go right back to the neighborhoods we tried to leave in the first place when we left to school." Anna's motivation as a result of his death was something I understood all too well.

Goal Getter

Anna's mind is always focused on growing and expanding. She recently began her podcast, Boss Basics Podcast where she interviews many up and coming entrepreneurs about their values and ideas. I am honored to say I was her first guest. We spoke about Urban X and a book we both read called *Rise and Grind* by FUBU creator and investor, Daymond John.

Anna has goals to one day take her multiple businesses international, and she is currently achieving that goal as she now has clients from the United Kingdom. Her story isn't nearly completed yet, but I think her journey so far would inspire any young woman to become a boss.

Never Turn the Dial on Your Dream

Inspired by Ms. Diva

Sometimes following your dream will take you down so many paths that it will be rather easy to give up. In the age of social media and the boom of entrepreneurship, I have seen so many new businesses and passion projects come and go without any real evidence that they existed. Sadly, it feels like most of them don't go further than the initial launch post on Instagram. I'm not sure if the market didn't need their product or service, or if the person completely underestimated what it would actually take to pull off the daunting task of following their passion and being successful. All of the people you have met thus far within these chapters have exhibited consistency and grit to fight through the doubt from their internal monologue or external forces. Many are still fighting, they may pivot, but their mission stays the same. Urban Xcellence isn't always about the finished product, but the journey to success.

The next person you will meet has inspired me from a far for a long time. Amari, or Ms. Diva as her listeners know her, is a prime example of what it means to be relentlessly consistent, and a real student to her field.

If you were to meet her, one of the first things that will come to your mind is how much personality she has. She told me growing up that she was always looked at as the life of the party. Amari explained that even as a child, her family members looked for her to provide some form of entertainment whether it was acting out a scene or preforming the newest dance. "I'm extra. I always have something to say. It was probably just a little more respectful because I was a kid. And, yeah, I've always been an entertainer." So much so that she recalled her teachers cancelling an entire trip because she was sick and couldn't attend. Amari also isn't shy to brag about where she is from either. Born in Harlem, New York, she takes pride in the rich history her community has. She says it's "ridiculous" how much she loves Harlem.

As we spoke, she brought up things like the Harlem Renaissance, the world-famous Cotton Club, and the other aspects that made Harlem famous like the style of dress, dance, and music. This aspect of the community she holds dear to her heart, have always been instilled in her and played a large part in shaping who she is. It's where she got the name, Ms. Diva.

Once we sat down and talked, it was very evident that all of Amari's experiences are the total sum of who she is. They are what make her. Harlem is a very vibrant place filled with interesting people and an empowering history. As a result, Amari is a very vibrant person, who takes pride in knowing who she is and letting everyone around her know it as well. It would be difficult to not see the connection. Then I discovered through talking with Amari that eventually her family moved one borough over to the Bronx. She immediately noted that the Bronx is the place where Hip-Hop was born. As far as culture is concerned, Amari had the best of both worlds because she was born and raised in a community that fostered her passion for entertaining, then she moved to the epicenter of the most powerful music in the world, Hip-Hop.

Along with the community influence, Amari credits her mother with her love for entertainment, even though she didn't initially see Amari's vision. "My mother, she's a T.V. head. I'm watching shows like Entertainment Tonight, Access Hollywood. Little things like that made me have the love for the person interviewing, and then obviously if you watch a T.V. show, you're going to have love for acting." At a young age, Amari could visualize herself in front of the camera, but her mother wanted her to be a little more "realistic." This dynamic is not new with creatives, the people around them tend to shoot their dreams down before they can really take off because they may not understand, or see what you see. In Amari's case, her mother just wanted her to follow a simpler path, go to college, get a stable career and live your life. Her mom, Amari explains, never pressured her into living a life that wasn't her own, but she understands that there can be so much uncertainty in the entertainment business and her mother just wanted what was best for her.

Now as an adult, Amari can see her mother's point of view. However, back then, she was not trying to hear it and would do whatever it took to realize her dream. "My mother wasn't there for me. So, I used to go on auditions by myself. You have to be 18, so I was [basically] going there for no reason, they were sending me away." To strengthen the point to her mom, Amari would reference other notable success stories like singer and actor Brandy, whose mother quit her job to help her daughter have a career, or Tia and Tamera, stars from the hit show "Sister, Sister", whose mother did the same. Well, that never went as planned as Amari's mother would simply tell her that she wasn't quitting her job. "In my head I was supposed to be on some Raven Simone vibe. I was supposed to be on from when I was seven. I just thought I was going to be a child star and things pop, but it just wasn't my path." Now Amari's mother is her number one fan and tunes in to almost all of her shows. "I'm just happy that now she does support me. But as a child, it just wasn't it. She was not trying to hear me at all."

As a young, headstrong person, it can be natural to hear other people's stories and think you have to emulate them. Their path was theirs, and your path is yours. We hear about the outliers of the world like Steve Jobs and Bill Gates who dropped out of prestigious schools to start their companies and become mega successful, then we may think, *well, why should I go to school when I could do what they did?* We don't take into account all of the people who have tried to follow in someone else's footsteps and failed because they were traveling down a road that wasn't theirs. "You just never know. Entertainment is a gamble, so even if we would have did that, no matter how talented I may be or what I can do, we don't know what would have happened. There's a lot of snakes. When you hear about these things that happen to these child stars, [you feel some type of way]. It's a lot of things I learn, I'm like, 'Well, maybe it's the reason why this didn't happen'."

Amari noted that if she had done things differently that she wouldn't have been taught the valuable lessons that she needed to learn or met some of the people in her network.

In all of our lives, we experience an event, or series of events, where it seems like the Universe is trying to tell us something. Those events, positive or negative, for some people can lead to a major transition and add on to who the person is eventually becoming. For me, it was realizing I had a talent and passion for writing. I wrote a paper for my world history class in college and it was so tightly written my friend thought I plagiarized it. I wasn't even offended. I thought this must be great if she thinks it's from the textbook. Then that summer, I was the guest editor for a newspaper publication and that was it! I got the bug to write and publish my own content.

Prior to those moments, I had no real aspirations to do anything on my own. I went to college and majored in History, even though my father stressed that I should go for a degree in media or business, and I had a career goal in mind to be a curator in a museum. Looking back, I now realize that it wasn't necessarily a dream, but more so me being "practical" (even though curator jobs are super difficult to come by, but that is a discussion for another day). For Amari, it was her first interview, which happened to be with a legendary figure in Hip-Hop, Kool DJ Red Alert.

Pursuing Her Passion

Amari was a part of a summer program with the Harlem Children's Zone, and they would have many interesting projects. One summer, her instructors had all of the children perform a mock interview where they needed to prepare questions based on the person they are interviewing. Once Amari was made aware that she would be sitting down with Kool DJ Red Alert, she could not contain herself. "So I'm like, 'All right it's lit.' I told you my family is from Harlem and the Bronx, so I know my hip-hop history. Juice is my favorite movie, so I'm writing everything down, asking all my questions. Everyone else is like, 'Who's that?' I'm like, 'Y'all don't know who that is?' The *youth*," she said in disgust. I thought that last part was funny because at the time Amari was the same age as her peers, but she judged them for not knowing any hip-hop history.

After Amari completed her mock interview with Kool DJ Red Alert, he told her that she asked some great questions. It was that moment where she thought that maybe she had a future in radio. It was her light bulb moment you could say. "So, basically acting is my passion, but I have a personality for radio, which I thank God for. I wanted to get into acting. Then I found out that you could transition from radio into T.V." Amari referenced former radio personalities turned actors Terrence J and Lala Anthony. Both started out in radio and as interns, and then through hard work and consistency, they transitioned to television and big screen movies. "When you look at those people and look at where they are now, Lala is on *Power*, Terrence is producing his own movies, and he's on the E! Channel." She uses them as inspiration and validation that you can have love for both forms of entertainment and do both.

Amari also added the fact Terrence and Lala also looked like her, played a large role in why she looks to them for inspiration. "Representation in media is very important to me," she stated, "[For example] Queen Latifah. I've always been a thick girl, so seeing her with her confidence, remember her character Khadijah was the star of Living Single, and she always was *that* girl. It didn't matter her size, so people like her always influenced me." Although she realizes that she is her own person and has to walk her own path, it does help to see people who look like her, or come from the same environment as she does, "make it."

Once Amari decided that she would take radio seriously, she made the crucial decision to really learn and perfect her craft. It is a step often skipped by many people aspiring to do anything great because we see so many "overnight successes" that we think these greats woke up and decided to be amazing at what they do. We don't hear about the amount of years this person had to work, and how many times they failed before achieving success.

Local Inspiration

Growing up in New York City, Amari already had an advantage when it came to radio. Every day she had the opportunity to listen to legendary radio hosts like Angie Martinez, Wendy Williams, Miss Jones, DJ Kay-Slay, and others to take what she wanted from each, style wise. Today, if you listen to Amari's show, *The Diva Report*, you will hear that her style is all her own. Nevertheless, that came after much trial and error of seeing what works and what doesn't, for her specifically. Amari also learned about the technical side of radio. Me being ignorant to the profession, I didn't think about how important that aspect was to a radio host. I thought all she had to worry about was the topics she was speaking about and information on her guests — there was a lot more that went into the production.

To learn more about this side of radio and to also get her college degree (which mom was happy about obviously), she decided to go to an upstate New York School, but that wasn't her first choice. Amari explained that although New York City was in her blood, she was always drawn to

California for some reason. Many of her favorite movies and celebrities are based out in California, and she just saw herself being out there one day. "I just knew I was going to go to UCLA." The issue was the out-of-state college cost. Amari had dreams of living it up in Cali, but she also took into account how expensive things would be if she went across the country for school. So she made a wise decision to attend a college far enough to be on her own, but close enough so she could come home if need be. The only problem was her school was small. The only black people she saw around town were the people she went to school with, and the radio station and media department could not do much to elevate her understanding of the field and overall skill set. "I had to prerecord my show and burn it on a CD, and then give it to the station manager. So even though [back in the day] they had to cut they're tapes at a point, so it wasn't that old school, but still, fast forward to now; they have platforms like TuneIn radio. So, it just wasn't upgraded."

Amari decided that she needed to be somewhere that she could spread her wings a little more, and be at a school with a more robust media program and radio station. She set her sights on SUNY Old Westbury to transfer. This school made even more sense for her career choice because she was able to obtain internships and network because now, she was even closer to NYC. At Old Westbury, Amari could immediately tell the difference between how each radio station worked. At her previous school, she was working off of raw talent. She did not have a real technical know-how. "So, I did my very first show, it was called Soul and R&B, with my boy Self-Juan the Don. Because I love throwbacks and R&B, you can't go wrong. But, we were doing it on our own. We didn't know what the heck we were doing." However, once she transferred, Amari began to intern at the school's radio station and really began to see all of the different ins and outs that came with a radio show. The station manager was very strict and precise in what he wanted and expected from everyone who worked in the station, and that helped Amari get better. She started off guest hosting other student's shows, then created her demo tape and submitted that so she could have a show of her own. From that point, the *Diva Report* was born.

I was curious to know how Amari went about creating her questions for some of the interviews she does and how she likes to conduct them as well. I know for me personally, I don't like to have thirty bullet points with questions because the interview can seem mechanical, too structured even. After I do research, I like to have questions that can take the conversation in many different directions. Also, I'm usually a fan of who I am sitting down with so the questions I ask, I actually want to know. Even with me preparing to sit down with Amari, I knew I wanted her to do most of the talking because I knew she had an interesting story to tell that many people can take something from, regardless of what dream they are pursuing. Amari explained that she always aims to make her interviews a conversation rather than follow a question and then answer format, "because I want people to feel comfortable and I want you to tell me your life. I want to know your deep dark secrets without you even knowing that you about to tell me. So, that's basically what it is; if the conversation is flowing, it's going to go to another level." Most of the time, she doesn't even use a co-host and she prides herself in that. From time to time she may have a guest host come on and fill in, but Amari doesn't like to depend on anyone else to put on a great show. It is an impressive thing to see because not many people can do that. If someone was to walk in as we were talking (and disregarded the lights and cameras) they would simply think we were having a regular talk about what she does and how she came up.

Take the Reins

After being at the school radio station for a while, Amari decided that she needed to take her show elsewhere to do it on her own. She explained to me that it was nothing against the school radio station, but she wanted to do more and expand her pool of guests. "I'm from the five boroughs again, so Long Island is not a part of the city and it just was too far for me and my guests. I don't have a car right now, so it was a lot traveling wise and I knew I had to transition. So, I'm like, *you know what, let me break free.* Amari took her talents to a station that in hindsight may not have had her best interest at heart. Anyone aspiring to do anything will tell you all of the mistakes they have made in their journey, and Amari was not different, but she's learned from them. Her new station manager wasn't recording her shows. She would come every Sunday and put on a great show thinking she would build an archive, but once she asked for the recordings, she never got them. Now that she is at another station, she knows to make sure she crosses her T's and dots her I's before she even goes on the air.

Something else Amari had to learn about was the way some women in the entertainment industry can be treated. During our sit down, she never sugarcoated anything when discussing some instances where a male counterpart tried to take advantage of her hustle and eagerness to grind and further her career. "I do radio, so if I meet somebody I want to connect with you, period. What do you want to do, what you want to shoot, when you want to record? I'm ready to work." It is an unfortunate reality that women have to go through, but Amari is armed with her boisterous attitude and her strong ethics to combat anything that can be viewed as foul play. Networking is very important in the entertainment industry. Your level of success can be directly correlated on *who* you know, rather than *what* you know. As a result, Amari takes her network and her reputation extremely seriously. She's mindful of how she carries herself in public settings and on social media because she wants people to respect her and treat her like someone that is competent. She also doesn't expect any handouts either because she respects the hard work it takes to get to a certain level. Why should anyone else have to look back to help her when she isn't putting in the same effort? Instead of complaining or comparing herself to her peers, Amari just asks herself, "what can I do to be better?"

Every Sunday like clockwork I can expect to see a notification on Facebook or Instagram that the *Diva Report* is streaming live. Amari's level of dedication and consistency is motivating for me, as well as other people, because most people take Sunday's to rest or to get ready for the upcoming week, not Ms. Diva. She is up and actively making sure she puts on a great show for her listeners and viewers. To put her story into perspective, almost ten years after she did her first interview with Kool DJ Red Alert, she ran into him again at the DJ Global Spin Expo and he remembered her face. Amari made sure to tell him that his words inspired her to become a radio personality, which she said made him happy to hear. Then on January 20th, which is National DJ day, and happens to be Amari's birthday she asked him to come on her show for another interview. It was a great example of a story coming full circle.

Looking to the future, Amari's goal is to one day be a host on a syndicated radio show. I was a bit shocked because I thought with the boom of internet radio and podcasts, being on a radio station would be something of a step back, but she stopped me right in my tracks to clear up any misconceptions I had. "I'm going to always love real radio. No offense, the Internet is the Internet, but God forbid that shuts down; we're going to need that FM station. Because even before we had TV, we had radio." Again, I was impressed by how serious she took her career and passion. Amari also told me that one-day she'd love to teach the profession of radio. She had been blessed with many loving teachers growing up and she sees how it's shaped the way she is and would love to pay it forward by teaching young people who are interested how to get into the field she loves.

Until then, Amari aka Ms. Diva is constantly striving to be the best she can be despite what people tell her about radio. "I just feel like internet is more flexible, but a lot of people try to say, 'Radio is dying.' Radio can never die, not to me."

Reciprocate

Inspired by Myiesha Taylor

I think it is very understated on how much of an impact a role model or mentor can have in your life. Urban communities are filled with countless examples of young boys and girls who were left out in the world without proper direction, and many of them ended up in toxic situations like jail or worse. One of the questions I asked everyone that I interviewed for this book was who they looked up to, or who made an impact in their lives because I think it is important to show that no one truly becomes great on their own. The next person we will meet has experienced the benefits of mentorship and she has also decided to pay it forward by becoming a mentor to the students she teaches and young girls in her afterschool group, Myiesha Taylor.

When my father and I first introduced the concept of Urban Xcellence on our podcast we wanted to make sure people knew that to be an example of what it meant, that they did not have to be an entrepreneur or run a business. They could have a job they are passionate about and take pride in. Myiesha fits that mold perfectly. I don't believe any work is unimportant, especially that of an educator. Originally from

Mount Vernon, NY, Myiesha told me that although she was a very active kid and big into sports like softball, she knew fairly early on that she wanted to be an English teacher. My parents will be the first to tell you all of the different phases I went through when it came to knowing what I wanted to be when I got older. So to hear someone know exactly what they wanted to do as early as the 10ᵗʰ grade, and is doing exactly that as an adult, is impressive.

I first met Myiesha during her freshman year in college while I was a sophomore. During the time we were at school, I remember her as being very diligent about her work because every time I saw her it felt as if she was rushing to class or going back to her dorm to finish a paper. Not that she didn't have fun or attend any events, but Myiesha seemed to have a better handle on what was happening around her compared to other people her age. I just always had this fixed idea of who she was, but in sitting down with her, she told me that she didn't always have her focused mentality. "In the ninth grade, I wasn't necessarily hanging out with the best people. So then towards the ending, I would say the ending of ninth grade, I kind of encountered a mentor, and she really helped me stay on the right path, and I totally changed a lot." That mentor, who happened to be a family friend, worked in the College and Career center at her high school and helped Myiesha become more passionate about her life and take planning for her future seriously.

She saw the opportunity and became "attached at the hip," as Myiesha put it, and fully immersed herself in the process of planning her future. Through her connection with the College and Career center in her high school, Myiesha got to go on many college tours in different states and intern with her mentor in her office. By the time she reached the 10ᵗʰ grade, Myiesha came to the decision that she either wanted to be a child psychologist, or an English teacher.

During her junior year in high school, Myiesha encountered someone that would make her decision clear for her, and that was her English teacher. For Myiesha, English was already her best subject, but her teacher left such an impression that it inspired her to follow that career path. At one point, Myiesha's teacher was out due to her having a baby, but it was also discovered that she had cancer as well. While she was out, Myiesha was tasked with making sure the rest of the class stayed on point with the work they had to do because the substitute teachers' put in place were, let's say, less than competent. "So she would call me the night before like, 'Okay, I want you to read this page with the class. Then go over these questions.' So she gave me such a huge role in the classroom." The teacher would also allow Myiesha to tutor other students for state exams. Those opportunities fueled her passion for teaching.

Spreading Her Wings

When it came time to look into colleges, Myiesha knew she wanted to be far enough to live on a campus, but be close enough to come home if she needed to. SUNY Old Westbury was a great fit because their English program was strong and she previously attended Old Westbury on a college tour, so she felt comfortable with her choice. After all, being away from home would be a new level of freedom for her as she grew up with strict parents. She grew up living with her mother and stepfather. She described them as being unyielding at times. Her father who she did not live with, was also described as very strict. Myiesha often wonders what she would be like if she lived with him. Although she was away from her parents, the new feeling of freedom did not go to her head and deter Myiesha from what her mission was. "I had a goal, and I kind of had values not based on what they wanted me to be, but based on my own standards that I held myself to." She continued by telling me that if she wasn't sure within herself, she sees how she could have easily went wild in college.

Myiesha majored in Multicultural Literature and considers herself a literature buff. When I was in school, my major required me to read many different books and complete a number of research papers. I have friends that picked majors specifically so they did not have to read as much, or do as many papers. Myiesha wasn't one of those people; she welcomed it. She embraced any opportunity to read new and classic books from different parts of the world, and she also prided herself in being able to dissect texts, see what wasn't right in her face. As we spoke, I asked her what her favorite book was and she told me that it was the infamous classic by author Paulo Coelho called *The Alchemist.*

There are a few books that when brought up in conversation immediately invokes many different emotions and thoughts from people and *The Alchemist* is one of them. It's definitely one of my favorite books of all time, and it sends the important message that what you are looking for could be in your face the entire time. That is actually a perfect way to describe how this project came about.

I was looking for inspiration from a variety of outside sources, but I didn't realize how many amazing people I met along the way and how each of their individual stories could help others. When Myiesha told me what her favorite book was, those very same emotions came flying back to me.

After college, Myiesha almost immediately landed a teaching position at a charter school in the Bronx. "I didn't really give myself time to take in the moment and appreciate the accomplishment. I was just like, 'okay I need to find a job.' So I was on Indeed, applying to everything." She was thrown into the fire right after graduation with the responsibility to shape and mold young minds.

Many people who plan to go into a career of teaching, major in education while in college. There, the education department will often times have intern hour requirements where they will have to spend time in a classroom at a local school with real students to learn the skills needed to be an affective teacher. As a result of Myiesha not majoring in education, she started from a different position compared to her peers. One of her first challenges was working with other people. She had to deal with other teachers in her grade and people she worked with directly. For one period a day, Myiesha had a co-teacher in her classroom to work with ENL (English as a New Language) students. During her first year, she felt like the older teachers looked down upon her because of her age and experience. "They feel like they know everything, and I felt like it took away the process of me learning and taking everything in. So that was really tough."

One of the more obvious aspects of being a teacher, especially in the high school level, is classroom management. Teens will eat a teacher alive if you let them and if they don't respect them. If you look at Myiesha, you would think she was one of the students. People tell her that all of the time, but she isn't intimidated by the students at all and sets the record straight from day one. "So for me, from the very first day [I tell them] this is what's happening. These are the roles. And one thing that

I do is I tell them my expectations, but I give them the moment, every class, every first class, to tell me what they expect from me as well."

Another way she sets the tone is by not smiling at all for the first few weeks of school. Not smiling was a tip she learned from her 11th grade English teacher whom Myiesha still keeps in contact with. The students start off with the impression that Myiesha is all work and business, then once the standard is set, they will begin to see a much more fun side of who she is, "[my students are like], 'Miss, we always thought you were so mean, and you're the coolest teacher'." If you scroll down Myiesha's Instagram, you will see a few videos of her schooling her students on the basketball court.

So full disclosure, I have always had a different level of respect for teachers because I have seen firsthand how hard they work. My mother has been a teacher for almost fifteen years, and I can see how taxing it can be, but I have seen how rewarding it is because my mother loves what she does. Myiesha demonstrates those same qualities when she talks about teaching. As a student, it can be easy to see teachers as these beings that don't have any outside connection to the world and live in the classroom. I remember the first time I saw my third grade teacher at the mall and I couldn't say a word because it felt so weird to see her out and about. My mother doesn't let me forget that story, ever.

Teachers have the important responsibility to watch over other people's children and give them the tools necessary for them to be able to operate in the world. Today, their responsibilities have grown because many parents now task their child's teachers with doing more.

Before, the parents were the child's first teachers — that is no longer the case.

In Myiesha's case, understanding the value in teaching the next generation is very commendable on her part. Instead of looking for a career path that made more money, she chose a path that would leave a greater impact. "Since I was in high school, I always said I wanted to work with teenagers even though I was a teenager myself. It was just something that I always had a passion for. I wanted to help kids, whether it's counseling them or teaching them."

The Girls Club

Another way to make an impact on her students' lives besides teaching in a classroom is with Myiesha's afterschool mentoring program for girls. She calls it the best part of her job because she is able to connect with 13-18 year olds on a different level. She holds the program once a week and each week they hold forums about everything under the sun, "… we just have workshops once a week where we talk about different topics: self-esteem, self-love, self-care, healthy relationships, friendships, and sexuality, just everything." Her program helps these young women navigate through high school because it can be a rough period.

What is great about the program, appropriately named The Girls Club, is that Myiesha allows a space for the older girls to mentor the younger ones. It is a way that each generation can pass down what they learned and *pay it forward*. Myiesha's teaching style is different from how she mentors her girls. "I like to tell stories, and so that's how I like to start off lessons, with a story. I like to be relatable."

When any connection is forged between an adult and a young person, I think is it important that the mentee feels like they are talking to someone who can understand where they are in life. "So if I have a lesson, I set them up. I ask them questions or give them a scenario, and I'll allow them to see how that will tie into the objective for the day. And then that's the same thing with the Girls Club."

When I was a summer camp counselor, I was able to speak with many of the kids that had behavioral issues because I spoke their language, understood their colloquialisms, and was able to see their point of view. Working in the Bronx comes with a different set of challenges that her students go through just to get to class every day, and at times it does take a toll on Myiesha. She could be home on her own time and just think about a particular student and hope they're okay. "I have to kind of learn how to back off a little bit, and really, what you can do, you do. What you can't, just know that they'll be fine. But I try to handle it by giving them hope and encouraging them. And that's my biggest thing. And even let them know that there is a way out."

Myiesha still keeps in contact with many of her former teachers because she still finds value in their lessons, especially because she is in the same field. Even as a teacher she still remains a student. The most successful people in the world may be considered masters at their craft, but they are master students at heart. Warren Buffet, often regarded as the greatest investor this world has ever seen, credits his success to his mentor and former professor, Benjamin Graham. Dr. Martin Luther King Jr., arguably the most influential civil rights leaders till this day was mentored by his father, and also by a man named Benjamin E. Mays. Rarely do you hear about a successful person who didn't have at least one person who was smarter and wiser than they were to help guide them in the right direction and hold them accountable.

This past school year, the Girls Club had fifty students who participated in the program. The first year of the program she was admittedly inconsistent because her duties as a teacher and mentor overwhelmed her. While she was passionate about the work she did with the Girls Club, she felt like she still had much to learn as a teacher first. She sees the program getting better and better every year. In the future, Myiesha plans to open up her own youth organization. She is currently finishing up a master's program in Child Youth and Family Studies, with a concentration on youth development. Once she graduates, she will earn a certification in youth development and evaluation.

Myiesha Loves the Kids

I asked Myiesha if she ever wanted to become an assistant principal or principal of a school and she gave a resounding, no. "So at first, the goal was to teach for some years, and then become a principal or assistant principal. However, now, definitely not. I see the work that goes into it and I just don't think I would be 100% passionate about it because I need that one-on-one with the kids." Myiesha isn't necessarily afraid of the administrative work, but she gets more out of having a more hands-on approach with the students. Her favorite part of teaching is how much she learns from them:

Honestly, my favorite part about it is, and it might sound selfish, is that I learn from it the most. Although I'm the one teaching them and putting all the lessons together, they actually teach me because they force me to look inside myself and to see things that may not necessarily be apparent. And they allow me to evaluate my past and really grow from my past, too. So I feel like that's the best part, being able to see myself through them and help myself currently.

In the future, Myiesha has a plan to put on a large-scale youth conference for girls called the Live Fearlessly Conference. She will have different sessions where everyone is going to talk about the things that young women go through, and things that they need more guidance on like mental health and financial literacy. The conference will also act like a networking event. The attendees will be fed lunch and they will be able to see other women of color who are successful, and see the different career paths that are available to them.

Teaching and mentoring can be very draining mentally as you have to give up some of yourself for the people you are working with. To help, Myiesha writes in her journal every day on her way to work, it is a way to release her thoughts and recharge herself before she starts another day. I wanted to know what she's learned the most about herself through this process and she told me that she had no idea the capacity she had for her students until she became a teacher. "I've learned that I am way more compassionate than I thought. Not to think that I was a jerk or anything, but I never knew, and these kids have expanded my heart in ways that I never even knew was possible."

Myiesha recently just completed her third year as a teacher and during an end of the year ceremony, she was awarded teacher of the year. It's work from people like her that sets the next generation up for success and helps make the world a better place. I am positive that Myiesha's impact will be felt years into the future because of the work she does now, one student at a time.

"Because My Muva Said So"

Inspired by Tia Monai

At some point, I think it is natural that we all look for a sense of community, somewhere we can feel comfortable and feel like we belong. This can be especially true when embarking on a new journey. Unfamiliar terrain can be easier to navigate when you see others are having the same experiences. It was because of this feeling that Tia Monai decided to create a community of her own called Millennial Muvas, a safe space where new mothers could discuss what they were going through, share resources, and also be a part of a tribe of other mothers who may be having the same challenges. Tia's motivation for creating a community of other mothers is a bit more personal, as she lost her own mother to cancer at a young age. Although her father did all he could raising her, without her mom, she missed out on many key moments of guidance and wisdom that could have helped her on her own journey of becoming a mom. As a result of not having her mother as an on-call advisor,

Tia turned inward with her personal mommy blog, then outward with the creation of Millennial Muvas.

I met Tia my junior year of college through a mutual friend. We'd had seen each other around campus plenty of times, but never spoke to each other directly. Once we did, we connected over an immense number of topics that ranged to music, literature, and your standard dose of what we called "ratchetness." Personally, anytime I meet a person who I find to be well-rounded, I am able to connect with them because I can have a meaningful conversation that can get pulled in many different directions seamlessly. For Tia and I, a conversation that started about who our favorite rappers were (50 Cent and Rick Ross), somehow turned into us discussing our college majors, then our career paths, then went into if we believed in astrology because we discovered our birthdays were a day apart. Ever since I met her, she has grown to be somewhat of a big sister to me.

We have been in a group chat with about four other friends since 2014 where we share news with each other, debate just about everything, and share funny memes and moments. Within the group, we've naturally cultivated our own relationship. Tia is very funny, and always willing to listen and hear what I have to say. However, she is also always ready to give me the honest truth no matter how I feel about it. It is a quality you grow to appreciate as you are on a journey of growth and self-development.

When I made the statement to my father and stepmother that my friends were dope, Tia was definitely included. I had just witnessed her get through a tough pregnancy that tested her physical health, mental wellbeing, and showed her who was really in her corner. Out of what seemed like a negative situation, she created something in

Millennial Muvas that has become bigger than just her. It was an idea that came out of desperation of wanting help. It was also formed so other mothers who were deemed "young" could feel valued, and like someone somewhere was listening.

When I decided on the concept for this book, it felt like a coincidence that so many people around me fit what I was looking for so perfectly, even though by definition Urban Xcellence is anything but.

I reached out to Tia for the interview and we made plans for her to meet me at my father's home to film after she had gotten off of work one Friday. She told me that she would need some time because she wanted to drop her daughter, Aya, with a babysitter.

On the day of our interview I text her to make sure our plans were still solidified, and Tia told me she was unable to get someone to hold Aya and that she would have to bring her along. She asked me if it would ruin the interview. Almost immediately I responded something along the lines of "of course not!" I thought having Aya (who wasn't even one at the time) sit in with us as we talk about the way she in large part changed Tia's life would be perfect and only add to our discussion, no matter how fussy she might get (and she did). Her being with Tia, in matching mommy and daughter shirts bought Tia's story full circle and fully demonstrated yet another angle of Urban Xcellence.

Born and raised in the Park Slope area in Brooklyn, New York, Tia described herself as your typical poster child. She did well in school, participated in beauty pageants, and had a textbook family dynamic where her parents played what she called standard gender roles. "My dad was the breadwinner, and the disciplinarian. My mom was the understanding one. Mom did the dishes, and dad took out the trash." When I first asked Tia about her upbringing, she mentioned that when she tells people she is from Brooklyn people expect her to be from a rough area. She then joked that she is from the boujee part and lived in a nice brownstone home, with both of her parents and two older brothers.

When Tia was thirteen, her life changed drastically. Tia's mom passed away due to cancer in her entire abdomen. Initially, the cancer was thought to be only on her gallbladder, and it was removed as a result. Then it was discovered that because the gallbladder sits on top of the liver, the cancer had spread there as well. After going to chemotherapy for liver cancer, Tia's mother went into remission for about eight months. In that time, she did not go in for regular checks ups because she was thought to be getting better. It wasn't until they returned to the doctor that they were informed that the cancer had spread to her other organs. "At that point, they gave her about six months to live, and she lived for about another like four or five months."

Tia acknowledges the mental and emotional toll her mom's death had on her family, and her in particular. "After my mom passed, that's when I kind of really went into like my rebellious time period. That's really when I ended up changing. I started like getting in a lot of trouble in school. You know, cutting school, cutting classes. Because my dad was always a disciplinarian, and now my mom wasn't there to uh, interject, it got really bad at home." At the time, Tia felt like she couldn't go to her father with what she was going through. As a result, she told me that her home became split — her and her brothers, against her father. When she thinks back, she completely understands why her father couldn't be fully present emotionally after her mom's passing; she never blamed him because she understood how much of a loss it was for everyone. Her father was going through so much. She understood his pain, so much so that she thinks that she put his pain ahead of her own. "He didn't [just] lose his wife," she continued, "but also his best friend; they're college sweethearts. My parents got married right after graduation, had three kids; it was his storybook ending. He lost everything." Although she did her best to empathize with her father, Tia also had her own hurt to deal with, and she did not have a healthy way to do so. It is here that she contributes her rebellious behavior growing up.

To help deal with the loss of her mother, Tia attended therapy through an organization called the Gilda's Club. The Gilda's Club is a cancer support community that helps families who have someone who was diagnosed with cancer, or who have lost someone to cancer. Doctors volunteer their time to help families like Tia's understand what was happening with her mom. Often time's, people outside of the medical field have no idea what is happening, and many times doctors use medical language that can leave people confused. The Guild's Club doctors explained things in a way that was easier to grasp and offered emotional support through one on one and group therapy sessions. It was through this organization Tia's mother has been immortalized on the Internet. Her mom was cast as an extra on the popular television show "Sex and the City," and there is a scene where one of the characters, Samantha, is giving a speech at a breast cancer dinner. As she is giving the speech, Samantha begins to sweat profusely. Then finally admits that she too has breast cancer and snatches her wig off, this in turn causes many of the women in the crowd to get up and take their wigs off, and Tia's mother was one of them. Her small part was turned into a gif and had been shared many times online. I have come across it myself many times and was shocked to find out it was Tia's mom.

The Gift of Servitude

One thing I have always noticed about Tia was her passion to help other people. The first college she attended was Delaware State University where she majored in early childhood education with a focus on special education. She thought it would be a great way to help children with developmental issues learn in a school setting. It did not take long for Tia to realize that she wouldn't be suited for it. As required for her major, she had to log in a specific number of hours in an actual school to get a feel of what it would be like in that field. In her short time, she found out that in many cases "special education" is used as a blanket statement. "Like, I love working with people with developmental disabilities, and things like that. I feel like children with behavioral issues and then children with like actual needs do not need to be grouped together in special education because ultimately they have very different needs." Her sentiments were very on the nose as I often complained about the same thing when I was with the Department of Education in New York City. My mother, who is a teacher, has also shared the same complaints regarding what, and who special education is for. Tia grew frustrated, and foresaw herself being a part of a problem if she continued down this career path. So as a result, she thought of another way she could help children and their parents, through social work.

Tia firmly believes educating parents is how you change the world because they in turn educate their children who are the next generation. Tia is one of the lucky people who was able to find work within the field she studied in college. Her father works in the Department of Homeless Services and was able to get her in the door as an administrative assistant. She subsequently worked her way up the ranks and became a case manager. Through her work, she is able to create tangible change in someone's life. She noted, however, that it is unfortunate that it takes someone becoming homeless to be able to receive help, but she understands what her position is and sets out to do whatever she can for families in need.

Creativity + Passion

During our discussion, Tia told me about her passion for language. Whether it was writing, reading books, or listening to music, she found a comfort in words. Growing up, she always found a place of peace through her writing. Tia kept a journal and wrote poetry since the age of ten. "Good poetry since the age of seventeen," she quipped. Today, she chooses to express herself through her own blog titled "Bug's Life." Bug is the nickname she gave her daughter, Aya, when she found out she was pregnant. The blog was the perfect outlet for Tia to release all of her thoughts, discoveries, and frustrations she was having as she was going through this new journey of becoming a mother. The blog was also a way she could be as honest as she wanted and not feel judged because she could stay anonymous.

Her pregnancy was a completely different experience than what is shown on television or even what she saw from her peers on social media, and she felt like no one understood her. "Finding out I was pregnant, was like a whirlwind for me, honestly. My entire pregnancy was traumatizing. It's something I never want to do again.

It was not what they make it look like in the movie." Tia went through what's called anti-partum depression. We often hear of post-partum depression that happens after a woman gives birth, but anti-partum occurs while the woman is pregnant. To help her cope with what she was going through, she found solace in one of her first loves, and that was writing about it.

Tia explained that she was deemed "high risk" very early in her pregnancy due to her weight. At first she wasn't too concerned because her weight had never been a medical issue for her. It wasn't until her blood pressure began to climb that she started to feel the effects. She would get painful migraines, and a terrible morning sickness that she dubbed, "all day sickness" that prevented her from eating at night. During her first trimester, she lost thirteen pounds.

She was in and out of the hospital because doctors wanted to make sure they watched out for something called preeclampsia, a condition that occurs during pregnancy that can affect a woman's blood pressure. If her pressure got too high, her body would seize and the baby would be harmed as a result. To stay on top of her health, Tia had to take her blood pressure up to five times a day. Even with Tia taking as many precautions as possible, she almost had a close call fairly early into her third trimester. When she was 28-weeks pregnant, she went in for a regular scheduled pre-natal appointment and her blood pressure was so high they could not let her leave the doctor's office. She was transported to the hospital, where she stayed for over a week while the doctors did everything they could to get her blood pressure back down. They informed Tia that they would have to perform an emergency C-section and deliver her baby if it didn't go down. Naturally, Tia was extremely fearful of having her baby at 28 weeks. She explained to me that when babies are born that early, they're considered "micro-preemies," and have many health issues because they aren't fully developed. "I prayed, and I cried, and I prayed, and I talked to my mom, and I was just like 'I'm not ready, and [Aya] is not ready. Whoever it is out there put your hands on me.'" Luckily, the next day her blood pressure leveled out and she was able to go home. Her obstetrician told her that they would not take any more chances, and once she reached 35 weeks they would deliver the baby and not let her try to get to full term.

Tia vividly remembers the day she went into labor; she woke up and took her blood pressure, as she had become accustomed to do, and saw how high her blood pressure was. "I ate breakfast and I was like, 'All right, let me take my pressure.' I felt fine. So, my pressure was at 191 over 101. That's like extreme. It was to the point that I had my OB's personal number. I called her and then she was like, 'Well, don't eat anything and come on over to the hospital, and bring a bag because when you leave, you're living with a baby.' And that's what happened." It's ironic because although her blood pressure was very high, Tia claims she felt fine. It was a stark contrast to what she was normally going through on a daily basis.

When Tia first got to the hospital, she was by herself. Aya's father wasn't there; neither were her father or stepmother. She thought about what was about to happen and how her life would change forever as soon as her child came into the world. She thought, "I can't do this by myself." Luckily her brother and his wife ended up making it literally as the doctors were pushing her into the operating room and her sister-in-law ended up being in the delivery room as she was giving birth. Tia went on to describe what being in labor was like for her. "I have no clue what a contraction feels like. I have no clue what being in labor is like. I had a splitting headache. I was seeing spots." Tia had her daughter at 4:18am the next morning; Aya ended up being born at 32 weeks and four days. Because she was born at about a month and a half early, she spent 32 days in the NICU and was hooked up to a CPAP machine to help her breathe.

As Tia and I sat and talked about everything, Aya began to make her way off of her mother's lap and fuss. She started to make a bunch of noise so we had to stop the interview for a bit while Tia calmed her down. All I could think about was how far she had come from being born so small that she needed a machine to give her oxygen, to crawling around picking things up off the ground (which we had to take from her), to at the time of me writing this, walking and running. I also began to think about how far Tia had come to being a full-fledged mom. It was a surreal moment just watching her in parent mode and knowing exactly what to do when Aya began to whine.

Celebrating Baby Aya

The day Aya was born, Tia text me, along with about four of our friends in our group chat to tell us that she would be staying in the hospital for a while, and to respectfully not ask to see Aya yet because she simply wasn't ready. During our discussion, I asked her how she was able to overcome not showing off her daughter to the world initially. Social media controls our world, and Tia and I are at the ages where many of our peers and old classmates are having children and use apps like Facebook and Instagram to show their newborn babies to the world. "Personally, I didn't want the first image of my daughter in the world being hooked up to tubes, you know, I felt like my daughter deserved more than that." Furthermore, Tia felt the first moments her and Aya shared together were sacred. They were intimate moments that did not need to be posted for the world to see; her only concern was the wellbeing of her daughter, not how many likes a picture will get online.

After Aya was born, Tia was added to a Facebook group of mothers who had premature babies. It was one of the first reassuring moments Tia had that let her know she wasn't truly alone in what she was going through, although it may have felt like it.

The Facebook group is also what prompted one of her first blog post titled, "NICU Warrior." It was about being a mother of a child who was in the NICU, and how she blamed herself for Aya being in there. "I understand logically it's not your fault, but in the moment, it's like there's so many things I could have done differently. Maybe if I would have skipped the fried chicken that night, or I would have took my prenatal vitamins that morning — this wouldn't have happened." Tia used her blog as therapy to get past some of the damaging thoughts she had about herself as she was going through this ordeal. After writing NICU Warrior, Tia saw the reach her blog had because she was writing about topics many women have gone through. She saw that women from places like Guam, Japan, and Germany were reading her words and it encouraged her to continue.

In her blog, "Bug's life", Tia often wrote about her not having the same typical experiences other would-be mothers had during their pregnancies', one such post was about her baby bump envy. She has never been shy about her weight, she proudly calls herself a big girl who has always had more — "more attitude, more jokes, more friends, and more belly." Reading her post, "Plus size and Pregnant" was the first time since I've known Tia so see her somewhat vulnerable. She wrote about not getting the normal "perks" that go along with being pregnant like, getting offered a seat on public transportation, never having to buy maternity clothes because hers still fit, or just overall excitement from random strangers when she bought small things for her new child. She went on to write about not being able to flaunt a big baby belly because of her stomach never got any noticeably larger and rounder. These were nuances that came with being pregnant I had never even thought about. "Bug's Life" became a judgment free zone, and a place where mothers who felt like they didn't have anyone to relate to went because they now knew they weren't alone.

Tia's blog is what birthed the Facebook group, "Millennial Muvas." She explained that it started out with twelve members and was originally meant to be a mom hangout group. She talked about being the only parent out of our group of friends and feeling like she was being intrusive by bringing her daughter to certain places we wanted to go. She felt guilty in a way for having a tag along. In truth, we never made it a big deal and always tried to plan an outing where Tia could bring Aya along. That said, I get her wanting to be around other parents and their children. They have a different set of experiences they can share, and other insights that non-parents just don't have.

Before she knew it, her small Facebook group of twelve members exploded to over 500 mothers, or Muvas, who wanted a safe space. 500 mothers talking, sharing successes, sharing pictures, and even sharing resources with one another. Tia understands mom groups are not anything new, but what makes hers unique is that it was formed around the idea that young mothers in particular need a community of their own. "Mom groups exist, but what tends to happen is the older moms try to monopolize the group and a lot of the times younger moms get caught into this stigma of, 'you're just trying to keep up with the Joneses' or young moms are only concerned about what they look like, what the kids look like, and they only care about social media. You know, and a lot of the time, we feel bullied in these groups with older moms." Tia didn't like feeling as though she was being put down solely because of her age.

She appreciated the advice she got, but did not like the patronization that came with it a lot of the time. "I love the fact that you're sharing your experience with me, but let me have an experience so one day I can share it with someone else." No matter what they (young mothers) did, it was never good enough to get the approval of the older moms. You can see this generational disconnect everywhere — in sports, music, and even within your own neighborhood. Sometimes young people need their own room to grow.

Everyday Millennial Muvas continues to grow because women from all across the country share the same goal and vision, to be the best possible mothers they can be and be a part of a like-minded community.

More than Just a Platform

In early 2019, the United States government was in the middle of a shut down that prevented many people who were on welfare to receive their benefits, like food stamps. Many women needed help feeding their children, and Tia used her platform to give out some vital information. She posted an "old school" baby formula that can be made with some everyday ingredients. Since I last checked, the post was shared over 11 thousand times. The potential is there for Millennial Muvas to be something huge for Tia, and other moms around the country. Tia hopes that in the future she can take it on the road and connect with the other moms that are in the Facebook group in person. Because she can only be in one place at a time, Tia relies on ambassadors around the country who throw and attend events for moms in the name of Millennial Muvas. She also would like to host events like community baby showers where people donate items their baby doesn't use or fit anymore. It is just another way to pull each other up as they all have a common journey.

Tia's future goal is to become a motivational speaker so she can use her story to inspire other moms who may have found their selves in a position like she was.

I don't believe we have seen the crescendo of Tia's work with Millennial Muvas yet. Motherhood is something that will never go out of style, and Tia will be able to share her new experiences with new Muvas, as Aya gets older. She will continue to grow as a person and as a parent. As a result, her example of Urban Xcellence will evolve just as she does.

Strive to Thrive

Inspired by Theresa Aristomene

Try to think back to where you were five years ago, now try to think back to three years ago, now think back to last summer, could you honestly picture what your life looks like currently? Our journeys have so many twists and turns that it is honestly laughable when we try to map things out and get upset when something doesn't go exactly as planned. One of the main reasons I am so passionate about the concept of Urban Xcellence is because the future, for better or worse, is so unscripted, undecided, and unknown to us and all we have is ourselves to try and shape it as best we can, with what we have. The next person I will introduce is a great friend of mine. Theresa and I have known each other since 2012 when we both transferred to SUNY Old Westbury and have remained friends ever since. Like everyone else within these pages, she is doing great work in her career field, and she is also giving her time to reach back and teach young women how to not only survive in the corporate jungle, but thrive as well. The creator of Developing Noire, Theresa Aristomene, has seen firsthand that many of your life's plans may need to be amended because simply put... it's life. Already a goal driven person,

Theresa had to make a slight detour on her path when she was diagnosed with Lupus. However, as you will soon find out, her diagnosis only fueled her to go even further.

Born in Brooklyn, New York to a pair of Haitian immigrant parents, Theresa described her upbringing as very strict. Growing up, her parents didn't allow for much else but going to school and coming directly home. She explained to me that most of what she did outside of school, she most likely had to sneak to do it. When I asked how living with immigrant parents maybe differed from her peers, Theresa could immediately point out the level of freedom they had compared to hers. "You know, like if my friends were allowed to go to a party, I'd have to, like, tell my parents, 'Oh, I'm staying after school,' or something. And I'd just go to the party, too. I was always very different from everyone I know." Early on, she explained many of these "differences" weren't exactly very noticeable. When you're in elementary school there isn't much to do outside of your own neighborhood. It is when you get a little older, towards middle school and high school, that you want to really get out and get active in your social circle and when that doesn't happen, it can have some negative effects. Sure in hindsight you can call it the normal growing pains of adolescence, but at the time, it's everything.

As a ten-year-old, Theresa described herself has a smart kid, full of life, excited about school, and excited to meet new people. Pretty much sounds like how she is now as an adult. However, when I asked her to describe herself as a fifteen-year-old, it was like she was talking about a completely different person. "Fifteen-year-old Theresa was a little more bitter. A little more depressed." That caught me off guard because I know Theresa as a bubbly person. Even if she is going through a rough time, you may not be able to tell because she maintains her faith that things will be worked out. She keeps that same childlike excitement through it all. I went on to ask her why she was bitter and what was she depressed about. "High school's hard sometimes. And I went to a big school and I was very insecure, self-conscious, again, my upbringing was very different from my peers and in high school, that's where it plays out even more. And like, you kind of stick out." It did not help that Theresa's family was low income when she was growing up. At the time, she said that even though most of the people in her community had a similar financial situation, Theresa felt like it was only happening to her. This caused her to feel more ostracized by her peers because she didn't always have everything she wanted, and she also had to think about a career in terms of what would pay, rather than what would make her happy. It was difficult to think about.

Theresa had to find herself, and that came with learning many valuable lessons along the way. One of the lessons she had to learn was never to let other people project their own doubt on to her. Theresa is not alone. Many people grew up passionate about one thing or one activity and due to their parents or friends, abandoned it for something more "practical" or something that would make more money. In Theresa's case, it was a couple of different interests; one was fashion. I assumed that her only passion growing up had something to do with teaching because Theresa seems like such a natural instructor and motivator in everything she does, but she told me it was once her dream to become a fashion designer, but she let someone else kill her aspirations. She obviously did not follow through with her dream to become a fashion designer, and who knows, maybe it wasn't her true calling, but she did not even give herself the chance to explore it. "I learned from that time period that I don't need to listen to what people say. Even if

I think that they know better and they know it all; even if they mean well. Like, if I want to do something, I need to go for it, [and ignore the] "oh it might not work out," talk put on me. I need to go for it for myself." When I asked if not becoming a fashion designer was her biggest regret, Theresa calmly stated that she doesn't have any regrets because she feels things happen for a reason, but it was her biggest lesson. Today, Theresa isn't too bummed out about not becoming a fashion designer because she figured out other ways to use her talents in impactful ways.

Discovering Her True Passion

Along with fashion, Theresa had another passion. This one has stuck with her since kindergarten. She's been creative in how she pursues it, even when people close to her say she should do something else. Theresa is passionate about unconventional teaching. At her first career job after graduate school, Theresa was an organizational development specialist who trained employees in hospitals about leadership and team building. She told me that she was always drawn to sharing knowledge and trying to bridge the gap between those who know, and those who don't. She's always loved school and can vividly remember kindergarten as a place that sparked that fire. Theresa had a great teacher, one who made it fun for her. "I came home one day, and I said, 'I want be a teacher when I grow up.' And my dad said, 'Teacher? Teachers don't make money; you can't be no teacher'." While this moment happened before the fashion designer dreams, there was something about providing information that Theresa just couldn't shake because it didn't make money, "So, I kind of like, shifted my goals, my aspirations, to different versions of being a teacher."

It's that knowledge gap I mentioned before that drives Theresa to teach what she knows and to learn more so she can then teach that. She looks at her own experiences when she thought, "wow I wish I knew that," or "I wish someone could walk me through this." Those words that she utters to herself only strengthened her resolve to fill that gap. For her undergraduate degree, Theresa studied Psychology and minored in Social Work. Theresa's career path is a perfect blend of the two, which can be a rarity for people nowadays who go to college. It is her passion to help other people become better versions of themselves. It is her unique experience that empowers her to empower others; it is like paying it forward.

Developing Noire

A couple of years ago, Theresa launched her personal blog and YouTube channel called Developing Noire. The idea came about after realizing that there were young women of color like her out in the professional world who did not know many of the nuances that came with corporate life and needed to learn. She and a classmate of hers, who is Mexican, would have these small moments where they would ask each other if everyone else go through something, or was it only them. If it were only them, they would go on to ask how they are supposed to learn how to navigate those confusing waters by themselves. One of the examples she gave me was how she dressed for work. Theresa knew she did not have the same leeway as her white counterparts did when it came to her work attire. "I obsessed over how I needed to dress for work because I was really trying to look professional, look the part, so that I can be, you know, perceived as, you know, a competent person. But my white male counterpart would literally throw on a shirt and pants and just walk into work. He didn't even have to think about what he was wearing."

I could relate. My first "big boy" job after college was also in a corporate setting and I felt that my white co-workers could get away with far more than I could when it came to how we dressed. I remember one Monday morning I came in and forgot I had my earrings in, I was pulled to the side by my supervisor (who was Black) and was told to take them out before someone else saw them. Then I noticed my white male co-workers wearing their earrings and rolling up their long sleeves with their tattoos visible, which I was also told that I should never do in a professional setting. I even saw some wearing jeans in the office. It was clear that I had to consider what I was wearing, and how I conducted myself far more than they did, and I STILL had it better than the Black women at my job.

How she dressed at work was only a small part of what Theresa had to think about. She often found herself second-guessing the way she spoke as well, "...sometimes I can be too colloquial, and I would wonder if that would discredit me when I'm doing a training." Again, she understood that she may not be afforded the same space as a Tony Robbins or Gary Vaynerchuck, who talk the way they want and even curse during their conferences and are called "edgy" while Theresa would be called unprofessional. You may read that and immediately think, "well yes they are in different fields and different levels of their careers," and you would be correct, but I think the point still stands. The inner battle Theresa was having isn't foreign to many Black women who want to simply be looked at as an equal and succeed in their field.

After years of asking these questions and having conversations with her friend, Theresa thought about sharing her experiences with the world in hope that they will help someone like her. She doubted herself at first, *maybe it'll be too hard, too much work*, then she quickly realized that she had valuable information and a much-needed perspective that many young women can benefit from and decided to go for it. "I was first conceiving the idea I was like, 'Okay. Theresa's professional development blog.' I was like, 'Okay, that's so corny. We'll work on the name later'." Through coming up with the name of the blog, Theresa stood firm on the idea that she wanted to target Black people, Black women in particular. She took me through her thought process as she was coming up with the name of her blog and I found it interesting in what went into it:

> "I'm like, "Okay, so, professional ... professionalism ..." the names were just not coming to me at first, and then I was like, "Okay, what about Developing Black?" Or like, "Okay. I speak French, I love French culture, Developing Noire," 'cause noire's black in French. so, I was like, "That's it!" And that was the name, and then I hurried up and bought a website and now we're going."

Of course, it wasn't as simple as coming up with a name and buying a website. Theresa had a new set of fears to overcome as she was getting her new blog, Developing Noire, off the ground and that was the fear of letting the world see it.

As she sat in front of me thinking back to when she had her doubts, she now sees that her fears may have been a bit silly. When I asked why, she told me that she was "being a punk for no reason." I'm sure at the time she had her reasons. Blogging, like public speaking, can invoke many feelings of being exposed to the world. When I launched my blog, Urban X, on April 12, 2017 (my mother's birthday), I was so afraid of what people might think of me that once I hit publish that I closed my laptop and put my phone across my room. It was my way of hiding. What's worse is that the site was ready to go live the week before and I still wanted to wait a little longer for things to be "just right." My first post ever was about the Jay-Z vs. Nas rap beef and which diss song out of Takeover and Ether was better (spoiler alert its Ether) and even after taking my time with the post and making sure I looked it over for grammatical errors, I still was not sure of myself.

Although Developing Noire was a professional development blog, one of Theresa's goals was for it to be a playground for her creativity. Since the days she dreamt of being a fashion designer, Theresa felt she didn't give her creativity the right soil to grow. She even had a personal blog in high school where she would write poetry, but she never kept up with it. Now, as a young adult with a new chance at creating a platform, she has a newfound appreciation for people who consider themselves creative. As a lifelong lover of school and education, even Theresa feels school can stifle one's creativity. She understands the stigma surrounding any profession that isn't considered stable or guaranteed because as you read, she had aspirations to be a fashion designer. However, once she told those same people about a career in criminology, for example, they weren't so quick to shoot those dreams down. Now with a career and a creative outlet, Theresa can explore both.

Diagnosed, but Not Defeated

After we wrapped up our interview, we stayed in touch and kept up with each other through text and social media. A few months after we did our sit down, Theresa began posting pictures of herself in a hospital bed without much context to what was going on. Her comments were filled with family and friends sending her love and prayers that we would get through whatever it was ailing her. I was worried about her because it had seemed like Theresa couldn't catch a break. During our interview when she was discussing that while majoring in psychology in college, she thought about what it would be like to be a therapist but thought it wouldn't be a great idea because she worried about her own mental health in dealing with other people's.

She then revealed to me that in the months prior to us speaking for this book, that she felt like she was in a very low place. Theresa felt she was depressed for a while. "People might not see what you're struggling with. People might not see, you know, those rough patches that you're going through. I don't know how many times people say, 'I see you doing your thing.' And I'm like, what are you really seeing? Because I wake up, I wake up crying, go to sleep crying, I'm not doing my best." Even before we started our interview, Theresa asked me what I saw in her to even consider her as an example of Urban Xcellence. I told her I saw someone working diligently towards her vision beyond the glitz and glamor of social media. I saw someone who even with a climbing career, thought about people from her community enough to want to create a platform for them to learn. I resonated with her plight and appreciated her grind. Even in college, I thought of her as a busybody, always involved and always with her feet to the pavement. In college she was involved with clubs, student government, and even Resident assistant at one point. She even told me that in graduate school she started a brand-new club, so it never came as a shock to me that she would be helping others.

In the following weeks, Theresa revealed to her friends and family that she had been diagnosed with Lupus, an autoimmune disease that occurs when your body's immune system attacks your own tissues and organs. She had looked up the symptoms and confided in people close to her that she thought she had it, but wasn't sure and did not want to self-diagnose. Upon a visit to a doctor, it turned out that she was correct. In the caption of her Facebook post, she spoke about fighting with her parents because they did not want her to talk about her having Lupus with people outside of their immediate family. Theresa stood her ground because she felt it was important to share her story and share her journey of fighting her disease. Lupus wasn't about to take away her identity. When she was first diagnosed, she was devastated and wanted to cancel any trip she had planned to a warm destination because one of the many symptoms she has from Lupus is photosensitivity, meaning sunlight can cause negative effects. She had every reason to give up and be a prisoner to this disease called Lupus, but she didn't. As a woman of faith she prayed, and prayed, and then prayed some more and put all of her trust in God that she would make it out of the other side of this difficult time. "Like, basically, the closer I've tried to get to God, the more my faith increased, and the less defeated I felt, and the more I learned about myself and the more I felt confident in what I was learning about myself." In a bold move, she booked a trip to California and returned home just fine. Maybe to her Instagram followers it was a simple trip to a nice state, but to her, it was proof that she isn't letting her diagnosis stop her from living her life the way she wants.

Since coming public with her Lupus diagnosis, Theresa has become one of thousands of people who are championing the cause for a cure. Her social media pages are filled with many inspirational messages for people who have

Lupus or those people who just need that extra boost to get through whatever it is that they are going through. Along with the work she continues to do with Developing Noire, Theresa educates her followers of what Lupus is and the symptoms some people can have. Lupus hasn't strayed her away from her mission, if anything it has given it even more purpose, because this disease affects many Black women. This past May, which is Lupus awareness month, Theresa invited all of her friends to join her on the Lupus walk that happens every year to raise money and awareness so that one day a cure may be found. I was one of many people out there rocking a #TeamTheresa shirt as we laughed, had fun, and walked for a cure. The energy was electric and full of hope. As I looked out, I didn't see one sad face. I saw thousands of people with their loved ones sharing in the moment together. Theresa brought us all together, some I haven't seen since I graduated and inspired everyone to do what they can to help. Her donation campaign raised over $3,500 from over 100 people and while Theresa was very grateful, she has her sights set on an even bigger impact next year.

Although her journey has taken many different turns that she wasn't expecting, Theresa's passion hasn't wavered, and her mission has been steadfast to develop the minds of other young Black women, to develop herself, and to thrive while doing it.

Seize Your Moment

Inspired by Maya Harris

Take a second, and just think, have you ever thought about the exact moment when your path, or journey was forged for you? At the time, the moment could have felt insignificant and unimportant, but in hindsight, changed your life. In many ways, that is what this book is all about. As I have stated before, everyone has a story, and it is important that we understand that our stories are just a collection of moments and decisions that make us into, well... us.

The next person you will meet has built an entire brand off speaking her truth about the moments that make up who she is, and who she is becoming. Maya Harris, creator of the blog, "Maya's Moment," and her podcast, "That Moment When" uses her platform to share her experiences, through traveling, wellness, and creativity. Throughout her life, she has come to understand the events in her life are the sum of who she is and is able to thoroughly examine them to piece together her story.

I met Maya during my very first radio interview to talk about Urban X with Trauma Radio Tuesdays with DJ

Skinny; Maya was his co-host. When I arrived, DJ Skinny, or Javied as I knew him, gave me the run down on how the show is ran so I would be prepared. He told me that he and his co-host would start off with a quick discussion about their week and anything interesting that may have happened. It just so happened that Maya had just returned back from California because she had won second place for an award that is given out to the best female radio personalities. She was so cool and collected in front of the microphone and I couldn't help but be impressed because up to that point I had never done an interview where I was the subject. I was still unsure of my voice and why my story was even important. Maya and DJ Skinny relaxed me through their calm demeanors and I was able to fully showcase my personality. After the show wrapped, I pulled Javied to the side and asked him if he thought Maya would be willing to do an interview for Urban X because I thought she was a great example of the individuals we like to highlight on our platform. He assured me that she would be open to it and I just had to reach out.

Once I did that, Maya and I set up a time and date so we could do the interview. It was the first time that I had sat down with someone who I did not previously know from high school or college, so I made sure I did my research so that I would have interesting talking points. The interview went very smoothly, as it felt more like a conversation. I find that interviews are easier when the person conducting it is genuinely interested in the other person, not just question, answer, question, and answer. When that happens, a list of questions isn't really necessary because the conversation can take the two of you in many different directions than what was originally planned. I try not to make that a habit because most of the time there are points that you must hit and questions you need to ask. However, off camera, Maya even commented on the fact that I didn't use note cards during our interview.

During our talk, she joked that I did not have any women writers on my blog and that I needed some. While she was right, I quickly replied that she was more than welcome to be a guest writer since she had her own blog and wrote about a number of topics. She agreed while laughing. While I was excited to finally have a woman who could possibly write for Urban X, I was more excited that I had added someone new to my network of "dope friends." We stayed in touch afterwards, sharing new blog posts we each wrote, and generally stayed up to date with our respective careers.

Maya was a no-brainer for this book. She wrote and openly talked about many of her struggles growing up and into adulthood. In doing so, she has inspired many others who find themselves experiencing the same things. So when I reached out to her again for another interview, I had to make sure that this time I went a little more in depth with what we talked about because Urban Xcellence is about the entire journey, not just the wins.

Born and raised in Bloomfield, New Jersey, Maya grew up in what she would describe as an extremely supportive household. From a young age, she was able to compare her parents to that of her friends and saw that her parents did a lot to foster a tight family dynamic. Even though their work schedules demanded much of them, they still managed to play a large role in her life. Maya's mother is a business owner, and her father is a truck driver who could be on the road for an extended period of time. She remembers putting on small plays in her house and her parents would be front and center cheering her on.

I was interested in learning more about Maya's childhood because she is biracial. Her mom is white, and her father is Black. I knew that her experiences growing up in a racially blended household would be completely different from mine because both of my parents are Black. I learned at a very early age what the societal differences were and the history behind them. Maya on the other hand, had to walk in both worlds without even realizing it. "So I think when I was little, I didn't see like my mom is white and my dad is black. Like, obviously by looking at them by their skin they are, but that's not how I categorize my parents." I was curious to how her parents taught her how to maneuver through both worlds because, as she even noted, there are certain nuances that go along with being Black or white.

Maya understands that to the outside world, she looks more Black than she does white, but also she told me that as a child, her parents never had "the talk" most Black children have growing up. The one where we are told the cold reality of how many people in the world view us because of the color of our skin. "There wasn't any kind of sit down, like a lot of black families have with their kids and talk about the cops, and how to act with them. I never really had that talk. I have that talk more now, because of everything that's going on, and I'm seeing it." She explained that her childhood was as inclusive as one could be. Although there are certain conversations that needed to happen, and they did, Maya said there were no instructions given to her on how to live her life because she was biracial. Her life was normal from how she saw it. "I grew up in a Baptist church and a Roman Catholic church, you know, one is done in Polish, the other one is done in English, So, I had a really good, well-rounded childhood." Today however, Maya is more aware of the differences now that she is older.

I went on to ask her how her friends in school treated her because she was biracial; kids tend to be a little less kind with their peers. Maya recounted an instance when she was in the fifth grade and someone asked if she was "more black or more white." To this day, that question still confuses Maya. She doesn't even know what it means to be more of any two halves that make up her entire being. I asked her if she found that her friends changed the way they talked about particular topics when they were around her because she was biracial. The conversation surrounding race has never been a light one. Throughout modern history, people have been known to be very tense with heightened emotions when the topic is brought up, and for good reason. The issue arises when you speak about any race as if it is a monolith. One of my closest friends is biracial, and when something happens in the news with race as a large factor, I catch myself and make sure I am more tactful in my opinion. If a news story comes out about an unarmed Black child getting killed by a white cop, I have to make sure I keep my opinion on the situation and not spread a wide net to all white people. I wouldn't want to make my friend uncomfortable. After all, he loves his white family members. And not to mention, I wouldn't want all Black people to be blamed for an isolated situation. Maya explained to me that she has a diverse group of friends who are open to have many of those tough discussions just so they can be on the same page, even when they aren't. It helps them have a better understanding of each other's point of view.

Growing Pains

On her blog and podcast, Maya often talks about the importance of self-care and mental health. She takes it very seriously because she herself has dealt with depression and even thoughts of suicide in her own life. Becoming a teenager is bookmarked as a major transition for Maya because she can vividly remember those thoughts of just not being herself. She remembers growing pains that she wasn't able to just shake off, and it affected her in a very negative way. One example she gave, on the outside can seem small but, when many small issues hit you at once it can do damage to your self-image, and at tender ages people may not have the tools to address them. In Maya's case, one of the first tipping points was getting her hair cut off as a result of a bad perm. "So, I had my hair chopped off in middle school. Like, I had really long hair, but it was like, I had a perm, totally not my idea, but, I got my hair cut off. It was like my security blanket." Without her hair, she felt totally exposed to the world, and self-conscious. She couldn't figure out her own style, and she just remembers feeling totally uncomfortable. Her troubles only compounded when she entered into high school for her freshman year and her friends all began to turn their backs on her one after another.

As a thirteen-year-old, Maya admits she did not have the communication skills needed to properly express her feelings. It seemed as if nothing could go right and, aside from her parents, she did not have a strong group of friends that were there to help her through her difficult time. She was bombarded with thoughts that maybe the way she was feeling and what was happening was her fault. She thought, "what did I do?" or "what could have been done?" She could not find an answer as to why people seemed to be dropping out of her life.

Her depression got so bad during her freshman year that she got to the point where she began to contemplate suicide. If it wasn't for a random phone call from a classmate, Maya's story would have ended there, fortunately it didn't.

One day she got a call from someone who at the time she did not even really consider a friend, and he simply called to make sure she was okay. He noticed that she seemed down that day in Spanish class and wanted to make sure everything was good. She thinks back to that call and credits it with saving her life. That call reassured her that there were people who cared about her wellbeing, even if it wasn't who she thought it would be. "It was this random person. You know, in the grand scheme of things, we may have a couple of classes together, but like we don't really hang out much, and then [as a result of the phone call] he became one of my best friends. I was a witness at his wedding."

So where were Maya's parents during this challenging period in her life? She has always had a strong relationship with her folks, so I wondered what their role was in helping her get through. She explained that she never told her mother or father what she was feeling because she was afraid that they would think they failed her as parents. Maya made it clear that her parents were absolutely not the problem; she just did not know how to effectively communicate what she was going through without them questioning their parenting. She was forced to think about how taking her own life would affect her loved ones and she couldn't bring herself to cause that type of pain, "…after that phone call I had gotten from my friend, I had like this weird premonition or vision, that I was in my casket, and I saw my parents looking at me, and I was looking into my own casket." While she thought about her parents and friends, she also thought about the people who abandoned her in her time of need, and who mocked and teased her. Maya refused to give them the satisfaction that they broke her. She told me that if she could go back and talk to thirteen-year-old Maya, she would tell her to do her best to keep the communication lines open, and that her parents will always be there for her.

Things slowly began to get better for Maya as she was getting older and finding her footing in what she was passionate about. She attended William Patterson University in New Jersey. At about the age of fifteen, she had the goal of becoming a journalist; she loved to write about sports and sought a career where she would be able to do just that. Maya would watch people like Cheryl Miller on TNT broadcasting live from NBA sidelines and could see herself doing the same thing. She also noted how important it was to see women of color in positions that she envisioned for herself. It was a subtle reminder that she could follow the path set out by other women of color, or she could follow her own. Maya told me that along with writing, she also loved public speaking and being in front of the camera. She thought of how she could combine the two, then it clicked — broadcast journalism.

I have always believed that college is a great place to figure out what you want to do with your life. You go in with an idea then once you learn more and have the experience, you are in a better position to make a better choice for yourself. Maya was no exception. Although she was really into writing about sports, it wasn't until her senior year that she began to realize that sports weren't all she cared to write about. "Maybe there is more to life than sports," she said. It came after much self-reflection that Maya decided that centering her life only around sports will make her dislike it. She was an athlete growing up, and if you go on her Instagram page right now, you'll be sure to find videos of her on the basketball court draining deep jump shots. However, Maya eventually decided to take a different route. She needed to rediscover who she was off of the court.

Finding Her Path

During her sophomore year at William Paterson University, Maya quit the basketball team because it had stopped being fun for her; in fact it was depressing. She found herself not even wanting to watch basketball on television because of how she felt. As she spoke about this, I recalled a moment in my life when a sport I played and loved, football, had ceased to bring me joy and I wouldn't even turn to the game if my team was playing. I stopped playing during my freshman year in college due to an injury. I had to figure out all over again what it was that made me happy. I had been playing football since I was nine. Every waking moment I thought about some facet of the game and where I could improve. I spent summers at camps and combines to get better, every day after school I went to the weight room and now, as an eighteen year old freshman in college, that was all gone and I had no clue how to fill that void. I didn't even know where to start. Maya found herself in the same spot, so she took advantage of her school's resources and went to therapy on campus. Through the help of speaking to someone outside of her family and friends, someone she did not feel judgment from, someone neutral, Maya asked herself a simple question that got a flood of answers. "What does Maya do? Well, Maya's a writer. Maya loves to read. Maya's a huge Harry Potter fan. Maya likes to go on nature walks." There was so much she was passionate about she just needed an outlet to bring it to life. The seed was planted for the creation of Maya's personal blog, Maya's Moment.

Initially, Maya stuck to what she was comfortable with and focused on writing about sports. It's natural to write about what you are used to when you finally have your own platform. Then, just as she did in college, she felt she was stifling her creativity by limiting her topics. Yes she loved sports, but once it began to feel like a job, she knew she wouldn't be able to breath real life into Maya's Moment. "It's a hobby to me. I enjoy talking about it with my friends for leisure, but to have a deadline, like, 'You must write about this, or you have to write about that'." When we met up for our first interview, Maya was in the beginning stages of reinventing her blog from only writing about sports and having the same old LeBron vs. Jordan debate, to a blog that showcased her other interests, like wellness, travel, and self-care. She also explained that it was important for her blog to be a welcoming community for people of color.

Once Maya began to write about topics that were important for her, she had no idea that other people would be impacted as well. She wrote a post on post-grad depression and how she dealt with it and the piece resonated with readers everywhere. "You know, we graduate with this twinkle in our eye, and then things just fall apart. Talking from personal experience [and] the stories I hear from my peers. Post-grad depression doesn't just hit the day after you graduate. Some of my friends, it hit six months out, once Sallie Mae was knocking on their door. For me, it hit an entire year after." It's not something that is talked about often, especially while you are in college.

Post-grad depression is very common among recent college graduates, and something I knew about all too well. We leave school thinking that because we have our degrees that our lives will be figured out. We listened to our parents tell us to go to school, get our degree, then get a job with a good salary and you'll be fine. That was the plan most people heard growing up. When that plan goes awry, a sinking feeling begins to seep in and you can feel like you are unworthy. I thought I would find a job in my field almost immediately once I graduated. Reality hit me soon after, and I struggled to find work I thought was meaningful and that fulfilled what I thought my purpose was at the time. Couple that with seeing my peers on social media who all seemed to have life figured out, it was a recipe for a lot of self-loathing.

Her blog article about post-grad depression was the perfect starting point for the new direction she wanted to take Maya's Moment. Her goal is to give her followers an inside look as she flew to new destinations, met other cool individuals, tried new foods, and physically did something for the first time. When you read one of her posts, you can feel that she genuinely wants to share her journey with anyone who is willing to take the time out to read. "I'm experiencing life through travel, tasting, and talking. So for people to like, want to be on that journey with me is amazing." As we talked, Maya gave a piece of advice to anyone who wanted to share their own journey with the world by way of blogging. "It doesn't start at your follower count, it doesn't start at the number of brands that want to sponsor you, or anything like that. It starts with just a community that trusts you, and believes in you, and supports you, and that can be like 2 people, to 200 people, to 20,000 people."

That Moment When

Along with the blog, Maya also launched a podcast called, That Moment When, with Maya Harris. It is a long-form conversational style show where the guests talk about the moments that made them who they are today. When she reached out to me via Instagram to tell me about her idea, I was naturally sold and excited for her. I was even more excited that she asked me to be one of her first guest.

For her, the podcast was just another avenue that she could use to inspire people. Maybe someone doesn't have the time to read an entire blog post, but they have time on their commute to work to listen to someone talk about what it took to launch their business or find their career. The podcast was also a place where her guests could feel free to be themselves. "People of color, we sometimes have to code switch or exist behind a veil, and sometimes we get lost in that moment of being someone else, or doing something else so we don't draw attention to ourselves. So what this podcast is going to do is just allow people to just be."

The episode I was featured on was titled "I love naps, but I stay woke." It was a play on how I described myself in my writer bio on my own blog, Urban X. We started off with the usual talking points — who I am, what I do, and what it took for me to finally take the leap to start my own brand. However, where Maya's podcast differs from many of the other shows is that we went in depth on the small moments that anyone could dismiss as unimportant. When it was decided that I would be coming on the podcast, I tried the best I could to script a perfect story for her listeners, but I couldn't. The questions I was asked forced me to think deeply and thus, I gave the most authentic version of me. Nothing was prepared. During the show, we talked in length about what it meant to be socially conscious while still remaining yourself. I see people every day get lost in what is happening in the world and they forget to do the things that help them remain them. I guess I have always been talking about self-care in my own way without even realizing it. It was a great experience for me and it was equally exciting to see Maya's vision come into fruition. I can only see her brand growing more impactful as she continues to create more "moments" for herself.

Maya's platform is making it okay to wear your faults on your sleeves in a society that demands your best self all the time. Through her blog and podcast, she shows us that every moment in our lives count, the highs and as well as the lows, because of what we can learn from them. It is an inspiring message; one that I feel many people can get value from. I'm sure she had no idea her hardships and her story would help someone else who may find themselves in the same mental space.

Falling Forward

Inspired by Marcus Rodgers

When it comes to Urban Xcellence, the process is just as important as the final result. When we hear or read about many of these famous success stories, we either gloss over the failures or they are omitted altogether. The last person we will meet has let his mistakes in business teach him what it takes to be successful. Marcus Rodgers is a perfect example of the phrase, "if at first you don't succeed, try again." I thought his story would be fitting to drive home the concept of Urban Xcellence because his story could be anyone's. To quote one of my favorite author's, Ryan Holiday, at any given point when we meet someone, they are at either one of three stages; they are aspiring to do something, have succeeded, or have met some type of failure. Obviously, no one wants to fail, but as Marcus told me when we sat down to speak, the lessons he learned when he failed made him more confident for his next endeavor. It is a quality that is missed in many entrepreneurs because society has trained us to think failure is the end when in actuality it is only more material to build a stronger foundation than the one you had before.

This story is a bit personal for me because Marcus is my older brother, and I can vividly remember when he was at his lowest point, but I also remember him pulling himself out of that dark place and becoming who he is today. I have the privilege of watching the strength of my younger brother, Elijah, whom you met a few chapters ago, and witnessing the perseverance it takes to be successful by my older brother Marcus. I'll admit at times it may not feel like it, but being the middle child definitely has its advantages.

Marcus was born in Harlem, New York, but raised in the Bronx for most of his life. Even though our old neighborhood is described as one of the most impoverished communities in the Bronx, Marcus said he had an amazing time with amazing friends. It was there he developed his street smarts, strong relationships, and was able to be a regular kid. When talking about his childhood, Marcus makes sure that he gives credit to our parents. "I had parents that had two different backgrounds. My mother, she's a teacher. And my father, he was not only street smart, but also book smart. So I had the best of both worlds." Their two distinct parenting styles provided a great balance growing up. Our mother is strict and structured; our father, more laid back. However, they both expected the best and raised us never to look down upon anyone.

Like most kids from our neighborhood, and most urban communities for that matter, Marcus had a fierce passion for sports and one day dreamt of playing at the professional level. Many of his friends and family, including me, always thought that his first love was basketball, but as I learned during out sit down, baseball was his first choice. I was surprised! If you see him play basketball and his drive to get better, you'd think that was the only thing he played. He was very skilled and could jump out of the gym. "I mean, if you were in the hood, the only accessibility is a basketball court. It's free. It's open to the public." He explained that he was actually more skillfully inclined, as far as the basic fundamentals of how baseball is supposed to be played than basketball. Basketball was just raw talent. Marcus played shortstop for our grandfather who coached the local neighborhood team. He doesn't like to say that he has any regrets in life, but he does admit that he wishes that he taken basketball more seriously because he feels he had the potential to be greater. Today, Marcus pays it forward by coaching little league baseball during his spare time.

Another one of Marcus's passions growing up was roller blading. He looked up to the older brother of one of his best friends who was a BMX rider and became interested because of how unique it was. "I looked up to him because it was different. It wasn't your typical basketball, typical football that any city youth are used to." He would start watching and recording all of the X-games tournaments, and going to the local skate park to practice his own moves. He got pretty good at point in time, too.

Inspired to Be Great

During his late teen years, Marcus began working for an at-home food catering company and got a peek into the lives of some very wealthy people. That impression stuck with him once he clocked out and returned back home to his neighborhood in the South Bronx. "I was observing people's lifestyle. And then I used to come back home [to my block]. Its two different worlds. I'm not saying I'm not grateful for what we had when we lived there. It was amazing. But it was completely different." Along with his catering job, Marcus began a modeling career where he would be around many influential and wealthy people. It would reinforce the idea that these people lived in a different world than he did. He told me a story of working an event at someone's home and his hallway was bigger than the entire apartment we lived in at the time. When he asked the man what he did, Marcus was completely shocked at his answer. The man told him that he owned the rights to James Earl Jones' voice. It's been years since Marcus had that conversation, but I could tell that he was still in amazement as he was retelling the story, "I said, 'wait like Mufasa and Darth Vader?' I had never heard anything like that before."

Since I can remember, my brother has had this itch for entrepreneurship, but I honestly never knew where it came from, and I never asked — but now I do. That conversation sparked many other questions for Marcus like, "what else can someone own?" and "why aren't we taught about these things in school?" His eyes were now open and he was inspired to start and own his own business. Any time I speak to entrepreneurs who have parents that are big on traditional education, I always wonder how they maneuvered. As I have mentioned previously, our mother is a teacher, so college wasn't even a debate, but he used college as a way to explore his excitement for business, learn more, and make connections that would help him in the future.

He attended a college in Nyack, New York, where he studied Business Management. While he was in college, he continued to get modeling gigs and he began to intern at a very well-known record company. "I used to drive my car all the way to the city. I have a book or casting call or intern at Atlantic Records. So I was doing that simultaneously while I was in college." As Marcus was getting closer to graduation, he focused more on the music industry, because he was able to forge many connections and got to see the inner workings at Atlantic Records. He wasn't an expert, and he'd tell you that himself, but he felt that he was in a great position to start his own business and learn along the way. The problem is that certain industries can be very cut throat and people within those industries can usually sense when a person doesn't particularly know what he or she is doing. "As soon as I graduated, no lie, like the next day, or like a couple days after, me and my former business partner started up my entertainment company." Marcus felt he was ready to get started, and follow in the footsteps of people he looked up to like rapper/ mogul, P. Diddy.

Whatever your feelings are about Diddy one thing you cannot deny is his work ethic and hustle. It is the qualities Marcus admired the most and tries to emulate to this day. Marcus' first business was a whirlwind of unexpected twist and turns, but he said as it was happening he was having fun. It was all new and unexplored territory for him.

First of all, the first business I had was an amazing journey. I mean the freedom that you have of having your own business is like no other. I mean, you know how people say, oh it feels like a Friday. When you have your own business, Friday feels like every day. Because you don't know what day it is, you know what I'm saying because you're in your own realm, you're own universe, you're own time. So that was an amazing experience.

His time running his first business did not come without growing pains. He learned very fast that people sometimes do not always have your best interest at heart and will try to get over on you if they can see you are young. He described the music industry as a "dog eat dog" environment that if a person can sniff you are young and naïve they will eat you alive. Marcus experienced a lot of the good, but much of the bad that came along with being young in a rough business. He was taken advantage of and lied to throughout, and it came from all directions.

His first major project was a music concert with R&B singer Trey Songz and Rapper Fabolous that took place in Miami, and on the surface the event was a success. Both artists got paid and the show was amazing, but what followed afterwards changed Marcus' life and taught him a valuable lesson in perseverance because as you will go on to read, when his issues were happening, they were his alone. Marcus found himself on an island by himself because his former business partner abdicated much of the responsibility of what followed and left him alone to deal with it all. Now that the concert was over and the spectacle was done, it was time to pay the investors back and when he and his business partner couldn't do so it caused many problems that Marcus could not run from. "I hit rock bottom. I wanted to be a little ant and hide under a rock. I mean it was bad." He went on to say that he could still physically feel the pain when he thinks back to when his world was falling apart. I was a junior in high school when this was going on and can remember how down and depressed Marcus looked. I would walk past his room and the light would be off and he would be sleep in the middle of the day. I felt helpless because at the time I didn't fully understand what was happening, I had no understanding of business law and how business even worked, but it hurt to see my brother going through it, and my parents really couldn't help past giving moral support.

Overcoming Obstacles

The way Marcus began to cope and get past many of the issues he was having was to read. Thanks to the examples set by our mother and father, Marcus found comfort in books and as a result he learned a lot about himself and his capacity to get through things. During our interview, I reminded him of a time we went out as a family to the mall to see a movie and have dinner, and Marcus told everyone he would catch up to us because he wanted to go to Barnes and Noble to pick up a book he wanted. As a kid in high school who did not read a book for pleasure and who only read required pages for homework, I thought it was so weird he would just want to read on his own. When I asked, he told me how much value he found in a lot of the books he read, and that I would understand. Today we compete about who has the better personal library and we trade books all of the time. I asked him what book was it in particular that really set him on the right path and he told me it was a book called *A New Earth*, by Eckhart Tolle. "That book right there changed my life. How I look at things. I became more observant, much calmer. Everything changed." He went on to say that book along with another one called, *The Power of Now* by the same author really shifted his spirituality and the way he approaches obstacles.

His transformation extended to how he treated his mornings as well. I have a love-hate relationship with early mornings. In high school, I lived over an hour away from school, so I had to wake up pretty early to get to school on time. Then I had a full day of classes, then football practice or I was in the weight room after school. Then I had another hour travel home on the train and I still had to do homework. When I look back on how my days were structured and how I was able to get up every morning without a problem, I am amazed because today my mornings are always such a fight with myself. Marcus, as well as most of the successful people in the world, has a routine he practices every morning that helps him put things into perspective and attack his day. He meditates for ten minutes every morning, then writes a list of ten things that he is grateful for. When he first told me this I assumed that the list said the same things each day, but I was wrong. He challenges himself to think about even the smallest parts of his life that he can be grateful for. "It's really challenging to think what you're grateful for because once you list the basic stuff — people, light in your home, a roof over your head, then you start being grateful for the little things. So I do that every day." After he writes his list every morning, he exercises, then he goes on to tackle his day.

The morning routine has helped Marcus tremendously because it makes him realize that although he may go through difficult times, he still has a life to appreciate. Marcus looks at the extra time he takes in the morning as an investment in himself. He asked me how he could expect to be his best self if he doesn't give himself to himself.

Failing Forward

Many times when you are experiencing failure, it can feel like a never-ending plunge, but once you land and survive the fall, you can come back even better. That is where I feel the beauty is in failure. I can learn and get better from this. When I played football and we lost a game, I looked forward to the hours of conversation my father and I would have regarding what happened. When we won, the discussions did not carry as much weight because we won. There are always adjustments to be made in success because nothing is perfect, but in failure, those flaws are more visible. Winning can blind you to that fact and leave you ill prepared to face any type of controversy. One of my favorite movie lines comes from the third installment from the Christopher Nolan Batman series, *The Dark Knight Rises*. There was a scene in the second act where Batman met the villain, Bane, face to face. During their fight Bane told Batman, "Peace has cost you your strength. Victory has defeated you." That line stuck with me because I understood it as how too much success can cause you to miss out on important lessons about life, and yourself. As Marcus was going through his rough patch, he made sure he was receptive to all the lessons life offered him.

It took Marcus a few years to fully pull himself up out of that dark place he was in. He flirted with the idea of going down a negative path to make the money he needed, but he was thankfully unsuccessful. He needed to find himself again, and it took a lot of self-reflection and honesty about who he was at the root of it all. The answer was Marcus is intelligent and very caring. He soon got an opportunity to work at an after-school program at a very poor performing high school in the Bronx. It was ironic because prior to him getting that job, Marcus never would've thought about working with children. From the modeling industry, to the music industry, to working with kids was a very big transition. "I was a Site Coordinator. And I started working with kids. I was playing basketball with them; just becoming a mentor. And what shocked me was that it was amazing. I had a lot of fun."

Marcus found that he very much enjoyed working with kids and being a big brother to those who needed guidance. Him being from the Bronx and working with young Black and Hispanic kids from his community meant a lot to him. After working as a site coordinator at the high school, Marcus got the opportunity to become the sports director at the Boys and Girls Club across the street. "I didn't know how powerful my position was working with kids until later down the line. I started to see myself in them when I was younger, and it helped me relate to them on their level." One of the first problems he had working with kids was talking to them as if they were his age. Not saying they weren't intelligent kids, but there is a different mindset from an (at the time 27 year old) adult and a seventh grader. As time went on, he got better and fully realized the position he held in many of these kids' lives as an adult and mentor. The Boys and Girls Club was a safe haven in the community, and that responsibility was not taken lightly. "The kids taught me a lot about myself and I will always love them forever. They changed my life." Although things began to look up for Marcus, he still had something looming over his head and it was the fact he still had to pay back his investors that put money into the music concert years before. He never wavered from his responsibilities, and it showed true character. Today, all of his investors have been paid back; it is an accomplishment that he is extremely proud of.

Working at the Boys and Girls Club as a director fulfilled a part of Marcus that he didn't even know was there. During his tenure, he introduced many programs and even started basketball tournaments for many of the teams around the city. He also held parties in the gym for the kids as well. Marcus' goal was to keep as many of the children who attended the Boys and Girls Club off of the street. Our father always told us that idle time is a vice, and where we are from, young people can't afford to have nothing to do. Who knows what kind of trouble they can end up in? Marcus was making an impact in his community, but he still had the itch of entrepreneurship. He craved the level of freedom that was allotted to him when he ran his own business, and he wanted to prove to himself that he could do it.

Midas Estates International

One day he came across one of the most famous business books of all time, *Rich Dad, Poor Dad* by Robert Kyosaki and it changed everything for him. It reignited the fire he had for business and sent him on a path to a career in real estate. What intrigued him the most was the fact that even after going to college for business management, having his own company at one point, he really did not know a lot about business. He also told me that it bothered him how much people just didn't know about money. After reading that one book, it led to him reading countless others, along with hours upon hours of research so he could then become an investor on his own. He was hungry to learn as much as he could. "What really got me going was the idea of building wealth and I began observing people like 'okay why does this person have that?' And what's going on over here? It wasn't actually the materialistic aspect of having money." For Marcus, he took into account where he was from and how most of the people he grew up with lived. Their lack of financial education did not allow them any real freedom, and Marcus wanted to change that and start to share what he learned.

The thing was, anyone could just repeat what he or she learned in a book without actually doing it. Marcus wanted to get out there and actually start investing. "You can practice and prepare all day till you're blue in the face. But there's nothing like going out there and making it happen. And you're not going to know everything." The self-help and business book industry is one of the most profitable because many people who read them never do anything more than that... read. It's natural to want to be 100% prepared and ready before making any moves, but that isn't how goals get accomplished. Marcus called it analysis paralysis because a person can be stuck trying to make sure things are just right.

Marcus created his new company, Midas Estates International.

The name of the company came about because our mother often told Marcus that he had the Midas touch and he plans to take his business international so the name just stuck. Marcus currently has his own investment properties and plans to expand his business even further.

I can say that I was front row to watch Marcus' growth. He is now far more confident in his decision-making, but he approaches each new challenge with a subtle stillness that allows him to take his ego out of the equation. He told me that he no longer harbors any hard feelings toward the people who may have slighted him in his early days because all it did was make him better.

Marcus has a rule that he doesn't do business with anyone who's never experienced failure, "... anybody who never hit rock bottom and they never made a mistake, and business is flourishing is 100% of the time they're lying." He wants to be in business with people who have some battle wounds (figuratively of course) because he knows if that person bounced back then they are someone he wants to work with. Is it fair? Maybe not, he says, but it is one of the many lessons that he has personally adopted from his time in business.

Failing isn't something to be ashamed of, especially as an entrepreneur. In school, there is usually one answer to the question and you are taught how to come out with that answer. In business, there can be a few different answers to a problem and many different ways to go about it. Mistakes are the steps needed to go further, and a part of the process to be great.

Urban Xcellence is about us giving light to the great things people from urban communities are doing, but it also is about the journey along the way. In the social media era, we love to see everything as a finished product wrapped neatly in a bow, but most of the time when something is great, it was tried and tried again.

Marcus has seen how bad things can get when something doesn't work out, but he's also seen his own heart in making it out and pushing along to something greater.

Define Xcellence

If there is one idea you have taken from this book I hope it is that no accomplishment is too small and that no story is unworthy to be told. As of the year 2020, none of the individuals you met within these pages are household names (yet); they are all works in progress. I guess what I love most about the idea of Urban Xcellence is that it is a never-ending process of looking for new ways to achieve success on your own terms. What does success mean to you? It is a question that I feel we should ask ourselves each day before our feet even hit the ground out of bed. The answer, whatever it may be, will guide you so that you know the decisions you make are yours and will only add to your happiness.

My goal in writing this book was to show that we are truly the sum of all of our Xperiences. It is both the large and small moments that make us who we are and what we aim to create. After reading through each person's story, I want you to realize that although we may be from the same type of communities our paths can take different turns. Everyone is moved to act by something different. Each story you read had a common theme, and that was they all had a passion and the will to pursue whatever that passion was.

When I asked what success or Xcellence meant to each individual I interviewed for this book, he or she each took a pause to think. If we were to use what we see on television or on social media, everyone would have said they would wish to have a lot of money and be famous, but that wasn't the case at all. Some acknowledged the importance of money in our society, but it wasn't what drove them. Success as well as Xcellence meant something deeper to everyone:

Yvette - *My personal definition of success would be being spiritually, mentally, financially and physically well in a good space and not lacking in any of those areas. I think success is about understanding your identity. Owning your identity and really knowing who you are aside from all the things. Aside from a title or a position; it's understanding how great you are just in your being.*

Dorian - *I will say, I don't think success is fame and money. I think that there is, people have moments where they were successful after achieving something, but I think, a successful person, is a person that is able to live a happy life. Like that is what I really feel like what it means to be successful. Some people maybe want the rich and wealth, and some people are fine with the nine to five. It all depends on your terms, but I think to be, to live happy, and to get through life and try to take the positive out of every situation and understand why it's happening. I think that is a real; that is a successful person.*

Elijah - *[Success] for me is trying to make sure that, like, your family is established, and they're taken care of. Making sure that you have the right, sort of, I guess, circle around you, try to uplift you.*

Andre - *Success really means to me is being able to look yourself in the mirror and say I gave it my all. It's losing or winning, but knowing that I have no regrets about it.*

Anna - *Success is self-satisfaction. I feel like a lot of people take certain concepts of life and they misconstrue it. It's like for example, when people say burning the midnight candle or that vampire life, burning the midnight candle does not necessarily mean not sleeping because you want to obtain success. It's sacrificing and different dynamics of life to obtain what you want to obtain.*

Amari - *For me, I'm just gonna say overall, it's not even career wise; success for me is being happy with yourself. Growing up I've always been this way. In elementary school you're talking about you want to go to Hollywood, you're from Harlem, they're looking at you like, "What are you talking about? You're bugging." So, for me being successful is doing whatever you want to do, making yourself happy. And that's with everything. Everybody doesn't have to be in entertainment. If you want to be a dentist, a doctor, a cop… Anything that you want to do, I feel like you should do that for you, because you want to do it. And your success should be whatever it is that you choose it to be.*

Myiesha - *I feel like for me personally, success is being more than what I was before, and it can be that the day before, two days after. It's just more …I feel like success is whatever it is that you have a desire for. And it's not something that's even for me, at this point, tangible. It's not even something materialistic. For me, a successful day for me is me having peace throughout my day and not responding to everything that triggers me. You know what I mean? I feel like there's levels to success. And for me as I get older, success becomes more intangible, and it's more things, inner success like in my response like healing. But then there's also success in terms of my career aspirations. So I feel like there are different levels to success.*

Tia - *My personal definition of success is just like waking up happy, and feeling fulfilled. Like, the day I can wake up and be like, "I'm so excited to do this work," regardless of what the work* *is, but I'm happy to be able to get that work done, then I know I made it.*

Theresa - *So, it's really being unapologetic, being at peace with whatever it is that makes you, you. If you're into sports, you like sports, you're doing sports, do you. If you're doing something or you're not doing what everyone else is doing, as long as you have peace in that... It's just doing you and, like, the way that you want to do you. You know? Like, in every facet of your life. Like, every facet of your life.*

Maya - *I used to think that it was having a good job, having good money, being able to live comfortably. Um, being able to live comfortably, I think is still the only part of that, that I still like to hold strong to. Um, I've had to come to terms a lot recently, that money should not be the reason you do what you do. Um, it's a nice cherry on top of your sundae, or star on top of your tree, but it shouldn't be why you wake up every day and sit down at the computer, stand behind a camera, or something like that...*

Marcus - *My definition of success. It's a good question because it's relative. My definition of success is cliché. But have health, mental health, spiritual health, physical health, to live the good life. It don't have to be extravagant. As long as the family's good. As long as you're good. You're living a good life and doing what you love to do, going through the struggles and all that, but doing what you love to do, then that's success to me. Yeah, that's success to me.*

It is my hope that you can return to this book at any time and find something within any story to resonate with and inspire you to continue to push towards your mission. Urban Xcellence is not about following a specific blueprint that is laid out by some celebrity guru, but it is about living and defining what it is for yourself. Take the lessons shared in these pages from these bold individuals and forge a path that is all your own. Understand why each of those moments you chalked up as insignificant actually matter in the entire history of you and realize you have a story is that important. Be fearless when stepping into the unknown; be stubborn when pursuing your goals; be resilient when faced with challenges.

Be Xcellent.

About the Author

Malcom X. Bowser, is a writer, curator, and founder of Urban X Podcast and UrbanX.nyc Blog. As a Bronx native, Malcom navigated his urban experience by being both book and street smart. He earned his B. A. in History from SUNY College at Old Westbury in 2015. He's been a contributing writer for the *New York Trend* publication and various blogs, he's woke, but he loves naps.

www.UrbanX.NYC
Twitter: @UrbanX_NYC
IG: @UrbanX_NYC

www.UrbanXBook.com
Twitter: @Top_Xth
IG: @Top_Xth